THE LIFE
AND LOVES
OF
GABLE

THE LIFE AND LOVES OF GABLE

by JACK SCAGNETTI

JONATHAN DAVID PUBLISHERS, INC.
MIDDLE VILLAGE, NEW YORK 11379

THE LIFE AND LOVES OF GABLE
by
Jack Scagnetti

Library of Congress Cataloging in Publication Data

Scagnetti, Jack.
    The life and loves of Gable.

    1. Gable, Clark, 1901-1960. I. Title.
PN2287.G3S35 791.43'028'0924 [B] 75-43842
ISBN 0-8246-0205-6

Printed in the United States of America

ACKNOWLEDGMENTS

The author thanks the Academy of Motion Picture Arts and Sciences, Margaret Herrick Library, American Motors Corporation, Eddie Brandt's Saturday Matinee, C. Carlton Brechler, Loraine Burdick, Enisse Chimes, Columbia Studios, Ernie Dunlevie, Dore Freeman, Charles Hudson, Los Angeles Public Library, *Los Angeles Times, Los Angeles Herald-Examiner*, Harry Maret, MGM, Joe Novak, Paramount Studios, RKO, Howard Strickling, Twentieth Century-Fox, Universal Studios, United Artists and Warner Brothers.

Contents

Introduction

CLARK GABLE wasn't merely a movie superstar. He was "the King" of the movies. More than 200,000,000 moviegoers have seen his 61 pictures. These films have been shown in theaters all over the world—from tiny huts with makeshift screens to lush movie palaces with the most sophisticated cinematic equipment. The films in which Gable starred (dating all the way back to 1931) have grossed a colossal $750,000,000. By 1960, the year of his death, *Gone With the Wind* alone had grossed $40,000,000.

In a business that reputedly discards old models as quickly as it finds new ones, Gable reigned unrivaled at the box office: he was one of the 10 most popular male stars for nearly three decades. Few have been able to capture and hold the imagination and affection of the public for so long.

Gable was the biggest star in Hollywood's biggest studio, MGM, where it is said there were "more stars than there are in heaven." In 1938, when it was in its Golden Age, filmdom abounded with great screen personalities: Douglas Fairbanks, Jr., Spencer Tracy, Gary Cooper, Humphrey Bogart, James Cagney, Errol Flynn, Edward G. Robinson, Wallace Beery, Fred Astaire and John Wayne. Despite this fierce competition, a national poll named Gable "King of Hollywood."

A list of Gable's leading ladies reads like a delicious *Who's Who*. On screen he made love to or manhandled Hollywood's best: Norma Shearer, Greta Garbo, Carole Lombard, Joan Crawford, Claudette Colbert, Loretta Young, Jean Harlow, Myrna Loy, Hedy Lamarr, Lana Turner, Barbara Stanwyck, Ava Gardner, Grace Kelly, Susan Hayward, Jane Russell, Doris Day, Sophia Loren and Marilyn Monroe.

Gable was a man of great charisma, but he was also a craftsman. It is true that whether he played a gangster, gambler, reporter or test pilot, Gable always injected an element of his own personality into his film roles.

Yet, after only a few minutes of any Gable picture, theatergoers were able to accept Gable as whatever character he portrayed. Film critics noted that it was Gable's *discipline* that enabled him to integrate his brash and forceful manner into the characters he played.

After World War II, when Gable reached his mid-forties and was greying at the temples, his legion of fans remained more loyal than ever, and his mail tripled. To his fans, Gable symbolized courage. He was an ordinary guy who triumphed over impossible odds. Even if the larger-than-life role that he played demanded that he wear a dinner jacket, or make love to a rich woman in a penthouse, his fans still saw him as a small-town boy. They admired his broad farm-boy shoulders. In all his years in Hollywood, he never lost his Midwestern accent.

While many stars were often targets of jealousy, envy, scandals and whispers, Gable remained loved and respected. He was admired not only by fans, but by every worker in the movie industry.

Despite his fame, his beautiful women and his riches, Clark Gable remained a "simple" person. He was never a snob. He always was a gentleman with superb manners, a man of great dignity, a man who never permitted himself to do anything that would tarnish his image.

He chose friends who liked him for himself, not for his name. In fact, many of his closest friends were not movie people. It would not be atypical for him to stop to change a tire for a stranded soul on a country road. He was a human being with a good heart who remained kind and likable through good times and bad times.

Gable's name was synonymous with masculinity. Women, young and old, relished his lusty self-assurance, and his dashing manner. Unlike some of the screen's earlier great lovers and suave actors like John Gilbert and Rudolph Valentino, who appealed primarily to women, Gable was popular with men, too. He was the very epitome of virility—a man's man, a roguish nonconformist, a self-made man.

Men found it easy to identify with Gable's real life activities: his love of fast cars, hunting, fishing, golf and beautiful women. And even after fame and fortune came to him, they appreciated the quiet man who was a loner, and who avoided parties. He desperately sought security, and perpetually feared that one day he might wake up broke and hungry. This, too, was something with which many men could identify.

Gable was a man who appreciated women—certainly an endearing trait. He would never let a woman possess him; he accepted their love only on his terms. He had five fascinating wives and many lovely sweethearts, and his relationships with these women offer clues to his personality.

This story covers the fabulous star's early years, his struggles, his achievements, the loves he won and lost. His was a life filled with the kind of drama equal to any that he was called upon to portray in the many films that he made.

—Jack Scagnetti

1
A Farm Boy in Ohio

CLARK GABLE AND MOTION PICTURES had something in common: both were in their infancy at the beginning of the twentieth century. Gable was born in 1901, just two years before the production of *The Great Train Robbery*, generally conceded to be the first real motion picture because it was the first to tell a story. But it was not until 1908, when films were being shown across the nation in store-front nickelodeons, that movie production companies began cranking away in the Los Angeles sunshine. By 1911, they had planted their studios in a sparsely-populated community 10 miles away—Hollywood. And while Hollywood was fast becoming the capital of the American motion picture industry, Clark Gable was growing up on a farm 2,500 miles east.

Clark Gable came into the world at 5:30 a.m. on February 1, 1901. The birth took place on the top floor of a two-story, white, clapboard house at 138 Charleston Street in Cadiz, Ohio, a small farming and mining town with a population of less than 3,000 in the eastern part of the state. The nine and one-half pound baby was the only child of William (Will) H. Gable and his wife, Adeline. William and Adeline (whose maiden name was Hershelman) were of Dutch ancestry. Will Gable (whose original name, Goebel, had been Anglicized) was the son of Charles and Nancy Gable. His parents operated a hotel and owned a farm in Meadville, Pennsylvania where Adeline's parents, who were born in Holland, also lived.

The proud parents named their child William Clark, and when the birth was registered at the Harrison County courthouse, the official records erroneously listed the sex of the child as "female." Father Gable was naturally disturbed about the mistake, and quickly had it corrected.

Will Gable was a Protestant, but he consented to have Clark baptized a Catholic—the religion of his wife.

Will had quit farming in Meadville and had moved to Cadiz at the turn of the century to wildcat in the nearby Bricker oil fields. He owned his own drilling rig and worked long hours. Adeline was ill much of the time after her son's birth, and the exhausted Will was burdened with the task of

(Left) Billy's mother, Adeline Hershelman Gable, who died when he was seven months old. (Right) Eighteen-month-old Billy Gable poses for a photograph in his home in Cadiz, Ohio.

caring for her. In desperation, he took her back to Meadville where her parents could look after her. Very shortly thereafter she died of epilepsy, when her child was but seven months old.

Baby Billy, as Clark was called in those early years, was at first sent to live with his aunt for a few months. Not much later, he was taken in by Adeline's brother and his wife, but a short time afterwards was sent to live on the farm of his grandparents, the Hershelmans, in Meadville.

Billy's father continued to work at oil drilling and in 1903 settled in Hopedale, a small town just 10 miles from Cadiz. There, he rented a room at the home of a Methodist family, the Dunlaps.

The Dunlaps, a well-to-do couple, had two sons and two daughters, all well educated. In 1906, Will married the oldest daughter, Jennie, a slender woman who worked as a milliner. They established their own home in Hopedale, and then Will travelled to Meadville to get his son.

Billy liked his new mother instantly. She knew exactly how to handle the shy, lonely boy and Billy found her to be one of the "kindest, most loving, tender persons" he had ever known. She gave him the kind of care and affection she would have given her own son.

Hopedale had a population of 500, mostly coal miners or oil field workers. Within a couple of years, Will Gable's oil work prospered and he moved into a two-story six-room frame house (the structure still stands), which faced a Methodist church. Billy attended Sunday School there, and his father later became superintendent of the school.

Will was away much of the time working in the oil fields, and so young Billy was left almost entirely in the care of Jennie. She gave Billy a birthday party every year, inviting children to share his cake and refreshments, and saw to it that he had a normal childhood. In fact, he was the first child in town to own a bicycle. Will always drove home on weekends in his Model T Ford coupe.

Gable's home in Hopedale, Ohio, where he spent his boyhood days. This photograph was taken in 1937 when the author's sister, right, visited Hopedale.

Jennie, a cultured, gracious person who loved to be around people, was a considerable influence on Billy while growing up. She taught him courtesy, kindness and respect for others.

In grade school, Billy was an average student in most subjects, but he excelled at spelling. He played the slide horn in the school band and was a member of the baseball team.

One of his best friends was Tommy Lewis, who had a sister, Thelma, a redhead who was known as the prettiest girl in Hopedale. Billy began escorting Thelma to Sunday School gatherings and other young people's social events. She helped him with his Latin and algebra and encouraged him to do his homework. In high school, they performed together in a play, *The Arrival of Kitty.* He played a roustabout and she played the title role.

Jennie tried to teach Billy how to play the piano, but finally gave up the idea because he didn't express enough interest. She, herself, often played the piano, however, as Billy and Thelma sang duets. Other friends also joined them at times and Jennie usually cooked for them.

During the summers, Billy often visited his father's parents, Charles and Nancy Gable, at their farm near Meadville. He helped care for the horses and assisted with odd jobs.

In 1916, at age 15, when Billy was in his high school sophomore year, Jennie became very ill and a doctor prescribed quiet farm life for her. Will gave up his oil work and bought a farm near Ravenna, in northern Ohio, just 15 miles from Akron. Billy helped his father on the farm, feeding hogs and other stock, forking hay and plowing. Many mornings he rose at 4:00 a.m. to do his assigned chores.

The Gable Theatre, named in his honor, was above a Hopedale garage, shown in this 1937 photo.

Already six feet tall and weighing 155 pounds, Billy looked like a typical farm boy, but he detested the work. He also disliked the daily five-mile bus ride to Edinburgh High School where most of his fellow students were half his size.

Billy was retiring and awkward, not very good looking, and not popular with girls. On the dance floor, he was all feet. But he did have friends. One of his Hopedale friends, Andy Means, visited him late in 1917, just before Billy was to enter his senior year in high school. Means suggested that they go to Akron to seek jobs because Akron was a booming town busy with World War I industrial activity. Billy seized the opportunity to escape from farm life.

Will was quite distressed when he learned that his son was planning to leave home. A terrible quarrel followed. Will wanted him to work as a farmer or in the oil fields, but Jennie sided with Billy and persuaded Will to grant him permission to go to Akron. When he arrived in Akron, he was a bit bewildered at first. Akron was the biggest city he had ever been in, and the crowds and bright lights overwhelmed him.

Passing for 18, Billy found work as a time-keeper at the Firestone Tire and Rubber Co. The job paid $95 per month, which was adequate to live on and cover tuition for the night school in which he had enrolled.

It was in Akron that Billy got his first taste of the professional theater. He had met two actors at a short-order restaurant and, in his conversation with them, he expressed much interest in the work they were doing as members of the Clark-Lilly Players, a stock company at the local music hall. They invited him to see their play. Billy attended the play, *The Bird of Paradise,* and was enthralled by the exotic costumes and the dazzling scenery. The spectacle amazed him.

Billy began going to the theater often, cutting classes to do so. One day, he summoned up enough courage to ask the management for a job, and soon after was hired without salary as a backstage callboy for the company. He immediately gave up his night school classes, but continued his daytime work at the rubber plant.

Billy's theater job consisted of running errands, sewing on buttons, and other minor chores. He received enough in tips to take care of the cost of an occasional sandwich, which supplemented the food sent by his stepmother. Quite often, he found himself hungry, but he was consoled by the fact that he was doing something he loved. Billy slept at the theater and showered at the YMCA. Eventually, he was given some walk-on bit-parts, and these moments on stage were satisfying and thrilling to him.

About a year later, when he was informed by telegraph that his stepmother was gravely ill, Billy rushed back to Ravenna to be at her bedside. She died a few days later.

With Jennie gone, his father decided to sell the farm and move to Oklahoma where an oil boom had developed. He wanted to get back into

At age 17, Gable worked in an Akron, Ohio tire factory and as a backstage call boy.

the oil business, and urged Billy to accompany him, but the young man stubbornly refused. His heart was in the theater.

Billy decided to go to New York's Broadway—a mecca for young actors—to try his luck on stage. But, with his limited experience, all he could get was a job as a callboy for a new play, *The Jest,* starring John and Lionel Barrymore. The play which opened in September, 1919 at the Plymouth Theater, ran for 179 performances. After repeated knocking on the door of the Barrymore brothers, he eventually developed a friendship with them.

When *The Jest* closed, Billy found himself jobless and began making the rounds of casting offices and theater managers. Unable to find a job as an actor or callboy, he ran short of money. Billy's lifestyle reflected it; he lived in a tiny walk-up apartment and ate sparse meals at lunch stands. So, in the early spring of 1920, he joined his father at work in an oil field near Bigheart, Oklahoma.

He was hired as an apprentice at $12 a day—good money for those days—but the work was hard and the hours were long. Billy now seemed destined to be an oilman, but he hated this life even more than farming. The harsh smell of oil was everywhere. Even at night there was no relief. The men who bunked down in his tent reeked of the foul odor.

As an apprentice, one of Billy's tasks was to clean the stills in which oil was refined. Sludge generated high heat, and at frequent intervals his job demanded that he be hauled out of the stills with a rope. In addition, he was assigned to odd jobs that called for wielding an axe to split firewood, or swinging a heavy sledge hammer. The heavy labor broadened his shoulders, but the work wasn't to his liking.

Gable's father was delighted that his strong, able-bodied son was working with his hands, but Billy had other plans. He had read a newspaper article about an actors' repertory company being organized in Kansas City and he wanted to return to the theater.

Disgusted with oil work after two rough years, Billy informed his father that he would rather be in show business. The young man had saved some money and, on his twenty-first birthday, received a $300 legacy from his grandfather.

Will fought Billy's determination to pursue a career as an actor. Father and son had long and loud arguments and, one day, in February, 1922, they abruptly parted on unfriendly terms. Billy went to Kansas City where he talked himself into a job with the Jewell Players, a low-budget but colorful acting troupe. He travelled with the company which toured small midwestern towns, working as prop master and general utility man, and he also played bit parts.

Too tall for juvenile leads, Billy later played a wide range of roles—character parts with whiskers, colored-mammy parts, and off-stage voices. His pay ranged from zero to $10 per week. But within two months of his joining the company, it disbanded because of financial difficulties, and Billy found himself stranded in Butte, Montana. With only three dollars in his pocket and a suitcase containing two worn suits, a shirt, and a few ties, he considered wiring his father for money, but he knew that Will Gable would pressure him to return to the oil fields.

Billy decided against it. Instead, he would work briefly at a nearby mine and then hop a westbound freight train. This he did.

He debarked from the rails in Bend, Oregon where he found employment as a rod man with an engineering gang. He then worked for the next three months as a lumberjack in a lumber mill piling logs.

Still hoping to find a place for himself in show business, Billy saved some money and in the summer of 1922 went to Portland.

He managed to get a job selling neckties in Meier and Frank's Department Store. A co-worker, Earle Larimore, also stricken with theatrical ambitions, landed a job in July, 1922 as the leading man with a theater group in Astoria, a town near the Columbia River about 90 miles northwest of Portland. Billy talked Earle into taking him along.

At tryouts for the Astoria Players, Gable met a beautiful actress, Frances Doerfler (who later changed her name to Franz Dorfler). He was fascinated by Franz who, at 22, was a year older than he, and he made it a point each day to leave the playhouse at the same time she did so he could escort her home. Billy confessed his love for her and Franz assured him that it was mutual.

Franz was Gable's first real love and he soon became possessive and jealous. Storm clouds appeared when Franz won a role with the touring company; Billy had been rejected. Separation was imminent. But Franz and Larimore begged Rex Jewell, organizer of the company, to take Billy along. Jewell consented.

Box office receipts were prorated among the players. Billy played bit parts and never earned more than $10 a week. The theater company did not fare well financially in Astoria, and it had to suspend its performances after only six weeks.

Left with nowhere to go, Billy and Franz were invited to spend time with Lucille Schumann, the company's leading lady. Lucille's mother lived in Seaside, a resort town 20 miles away and the trio journeyed to the Schumann home. Shortly after their arrival, they were summoned back to Astoria. The troupe was about to begin an ambitious river tour. The plan was to sail down the Columbia River, performing in little towns along the way. Franz and Billy returned to Astoria and rejoined Jewell's troupe. The company traveled on cheap boats without cabins. Even though it was early fall and the weather was often unpleasant, the company slept on deck. Again, there was little money for the actors. Unhappy with working conditions, several of the actors left the company and Billy soon found himself thrust into more substantial roles. During one week he played 14

(Above) Franz Doerfler, a stage actress from Oregon, was Gable's girl friend from 1922 to 1924. (Right) This picture of Gable was taken by Franz Doerfler in Portland, Oregon, in 1924.

performances—but he received only $1.30 for his work. He played a seaman in *Blundering Billy* and in *The Villun Still Pursued Her,* he was dressed as a baby and sat in a huge crib.

Billy and Franz grew closer during the river tour and became engaged. They were happy despite the primitive conditions.

In late fall of 1922, when the river tour ended, Billy was in poor health. He had lost much weight and was badly in need of rest. Franz invited him to her family's farm in Silverton, Oregon, where he immediately befriended her mother and father. He addressed them as "Mom" and "Dad," perhaps out of a longing for his deceased mother and alienated father. This time he found happiness on the farm. He had no chores to do and he had Franz to love. He asked her to be his wife, but she put him off. Franz worried about Billy's ability to support them both. She feared what poverty might do to their love, and she did not want to abandon plans of a theatrical career for herself.

Billy took a job in the loading department at the Silver Falls Lumber Company for $3.20 a day and moved into a boarding house seven miles from the farm. He walked to the Doerfler home on weekends to visit Franz.

Franz moved to Portland in November of 1922 to take singing lessons, and Billy continued to visit her on weekends, making a 25-mile trip. She soon landed a job with a new musical show touring the Northwest and the two were separated at Christmas time. Billy spent the holidays with her family.

In January of 1923, Billy quit his job with the lumber mill and moved to Portland. He obtained work as a classified ad salesman for the *Portland Oregonian.* Two months later, he took an office job with the telephone company, a position that he kept for one year.

Billy and Franz continued to correspond by mail. Franz learned that Josephine Dillon, a Broadway actress who had taught dramatics in New York was opening a small theater in Portland. She urged Billy to contact Miss Dillon. Hoping that she might find a role for him in the group, Billy heeded the advice. Josephine Dillon was impressed by the young man and invited him to study with her.

Billy's hopes of becoming an actor were renewed. Miss Dillon, after all, had an excellent education and was experienced in the dramatic arts. She had graduated from Stanford University in 1908 when she was 20 years old, and had furthered her education in New York and Paris. Experienced as a lecturer on speech and acting techniques, she was active in the Liberty Theater of the United States Army School during World War I. She came from a good family as well: her father had once been District Attorney of Los Angeles.

Billy's meeting with Josephine Dillon was an important event in his life. He had yet much to learn about being a good actor. He knew that he spoke poorly, moved awkwardly—and he knew, too, that Josephine Dillon could teach him the fine points of acting.

Miss Dillon felt that Billy had great potential as an actor. This, coupled with his ambition and drive to succeed, made for a good relationship.

Billy held Josephine in high esteem. He was certain that without her he would never get anywhere in show business. "Working with Josephine has come to mean everything to me," he told Franz.

When Billy became ill, Josephine took a special interest in him. She paid for a three-week vacation at a ranch so he could recover his failing health, paid a doctor to prescribe a diet for him, and immediately afterward arranged for him to take a physical culture course. It was apparent by now that Josephine was more than just interested in helping Billy develop his acting potential. Josephine Dillon had fallen in love with Billy Gable.

While maintaining a close, friendly relationship with Josephine, Billy continued to correspond with Franz, although his letters became less affectionate. He saw Franz whenever she was in Portland for her stage work. But working days with the telephone company and nights in theater classes left him little time, and their contact became less frequent.

When they met in Portland at a Christmas Eve party at her brother's house, Franz told Billy that she was now willing to marry him and wanted to discuss marriage plans. But Billy explained that he no longer loved *her,* stressing the fact that he was going to study with Josephine Dillon for the next few years. The news hurt Franz immensely, but on New Year's Eve Billy telephoned her and apologized for what he had said about his feelings for her, and that he would marry her. When they next met, however, Franz sensed that he was returning to her only out of obligation and that the original feelings of closeness were gone. Once again, she decided to postpone the marriage.

In the early summer of 1924, Josephine Dillon moved to Hollywood to open a drama school; Billy followed two weeks later. Within six months, on December 13, 1924, Josephine Dillon and William Clark Gable were married in a quiet ceremony in a church office. He was 23, she was 37.

The Gables rented a $20-a-month bungalow court apartment. Billy bought a used car for $50 and made the rounds of theatrical groups. Josephine helped him secure a few jobs as an extra in silent movies. His first job as an extra was in *Forbidden Paradise,* starring Pola Negri and Rod La Rocque. Josephine read scripts for the Palmer Photoplay Corporation and began recruiting dramatic school students.

At this point in his life, Billy decided to drop his first name and to use his middle name—Clark. The idea developed when he and Josephine were shopping on Hollywood Boulevard one day. They stopped to make a purchase at Clark's Dollar Shirt Shop, and she suggested that Clark would be an excellent stage name. He agreed.

Josephine also urged that Clark see a dentist. There was an unattractive space between his front teeth, and she felt it needed attention. He complied.

Each day, Gable sat at the piano for long periods of time. Under Josephine's direction, he worked for accuracy of tone. Starting at a high pitch and working his voice down, a half-tone at a time, his high-pitched, squeaky voice gradually took on quality and resonance.

"You can notice the results of his work in the amazing resonance behind his speech and the firmness of his tones," Josephine later said. "He had a conglomeration of vowels from East and West, from farm and city, from workmen and leisure people, and a scattering of Dutch. However, it was all virile, energetic and full of character and tone quality."

Josephine encouraged Gable to read books to further his own education. Whenever she could salvage a quarter from their tight budget she gave it to Clark so that he might see a movie and study the style of the screen's better actors.

Josephine Dillon was the only drama teacher Gable ever had.

Hollywood in the mid-1920s still produced silent films. Although thousands of people were employed by the industry, they were mostly electricians, prop men, carpenters, laborers and office workers. Many actors registered as extras. It was not unusual for more than 100 people to attend a single call for a job as an extra. The male film stars of the era—actors

Gable in 1925, a year after he arrived in Hollywood to seek work in stage plays or as a film extra.

Rudolph Valentino, John Gilbert, Douglas Fairbanks, Ramon Novarro, and Rod La Rocque, along with comedians Charlie Chaplin and Harold Lloyd, and leading western heroes Tom Mix and William S. Hart—had fabulous incomes.

Stage acting jobs for unknowns were scarce in 1925. Gable had never before considered acting in films, but having had little luck in the theater, he decided that movies might provide his best chance for employment. But the screen's leading men at that time—Valentino and Gilbert—were suave and romantic. Gable was aware that he was considered a rough and tough "heavy."

Clark managed to get a bit part in the 1925 film, *White Man*, which paid $15 a day, but only lasted for 10 days. He snared a few extra roles at $5 a day and one at $7.50 (for one day only) in *The Merry Widow* with Mae Murray and John Gilbert. He was a spear carrier in *Romeo and Juliet* crowd scenes in the summer of 1925 for the West Coast Road Company. The production was directed by Lillian Albertson and produced by Louis O. Macloon, a husband-and-wife team. He received $35 per week, and an invitation to the hotel room of Broadway actress Jane Cowl, 39, a member of the company. She had eyes for Gable and soon helped him get a bigger role. With her help, later that year, he appeared in the company's production of *What Price Glory?* He was initially cast as a roughneck soldier, but later played the meatier role of Sergeant Quirt. After that, he appeared in six other plays, mostly in minor roles. His affair with Jane Cowl was obviously not one of the heart, but a means of advancing himself in the theater. The relationship lasted for a short time. Gable was, after all, a married man.

In the summer of 1926, Lionel Barrymore, who remembered Gable from his callboy days in New York, hired him for a Los Angeles production of *Copperhead*. All did not go smoothly. Gable was reprimanded by Lionel, who not only starred in, but directed the production. Clark had clumsily dropped his hat into a "deep well" on stage, and when he quickly bent over and reached down to retrieve it, the audience roared.

Times were tough for Clark. He and Josephine lived modestly. She supplemented their meager income by working at odd jobs and by instructing private students. She also took care of all household chores—cooking, cleaning, shopping, ironing and mending clothes.

Busy as she was, Josephine still devoted much time to helping Clark develop his craft as an actor. Their relationship seemed more teacher-and-pupil than husband-and-wife. Clark began to resent her relentless instructions and domineering attitude.

The Gable marriage started to deteriorate. In 1926, when Pauline Frederick, a 39-year-old actress, got him a role in her *Madame X* stage play, he accepted an invitation to visit her apartment each night after the show. This affair, like the brief one with Jane Cowl, ended with the closing of the play. When Josephine learned of the encounter, Gable moved into a furnished room by himself. But Josephine was very tolerant of his affairs. The women had pursued him, she believed. He could not be truly held responsible.

Gable's biggest role came when he was cast as a reporter in a Hollywood stock company production of *Chicago* in the spring of 1927. *Chicago*, starring Nancy Carroll, played for several weeks at the Music Box on Hollywood Boulevard. Gable was spotted there by a talent scout from a Houston, Texas stock company. He was offered a job in Houston as a second man in the company. He took it. Josephine remained in Hollywood teaching drama.

After 14 weeks in Houston, Gable found himself playing leads, and earning a salary of $75 per week. When the Houston stock season ended, he followed other members of the stock company to New York.

In the fall of 1928, Gable appeared for 16 weeks in *Machinal* at Broadway's Plymouth Theater (where he had been a callboy years before) and won favorable reviews. *The New York Times* commented that Gable "played the casual, good-humored lover without a hackneyed gesture." The *Morning Telegraph* said: "He (Gable) is young, vigorous, and brutally masculine."

Josephine Dillon, Gable's first wife, is shown in 1930 at the time of their divorce. She was his first and only drama teacher.

Josephine visited Gable in New York during that winter of 1929 and urged him to return to California. He refused. There was no future for him in films, he told her. Having come to the realization that her relationship with Gable could not be salvaged, Josephine Dillon returned to California and, in March of 1929, filed for divorce.

After *Machinal,* Gable appeared in four other plays, all short runs. He was judged a competent actor, but received no special recognition.

Finding work on the Broadway stage or anywhere else was difficult. The stock market had crashed and the nation's economy was waning. What few stage jobs were available were awarded to upcoming actors of promise and competence—Jimmy Cagney, Paul Muni, Humphrey Bogart, Edward G. Robinson, Fredric March, Robert Montgomery, Spencer Tracy, Pat O'Brien and Burgess Meredith—all of whom later became famous movie stars. Unknowns had to wait and hope.

While out of work in New York, Gable spent many days making the rounds of casting offices. Some evenings he bought cheap balcony seats to Broadway plays so he could see other actors work and study their techniques. He spent many evenings in night court studying the wide variety of people arrested for such crimes as pickpocketing, burglary, drunkenness, prostitution and pimping. He knew that the more he studied life, the more it would enhance his art. He also read and studied the history of the theater.

Being without work for several months during the latter part of 1929 and early 1930, Gable found himself running short of funds. Once again, he found himself at a crossroads and he pondered which way to turn. Should he return to Hollywood, or should he stick it out in New York?

2

Ria Langham, Socialite Wife

WHILE IN NEW YORK BETWEEN 1928 and 1930, Gable spent much time in the company of Ria Langham, a wealthy socialite. They had met in September, 1928, when he was appearing in *Machinal.* Ria, a resident of Houston, was in New York visiting her teenage daughter who was attending a finishing school in Westchester County. Ria had seen Gable once before—when he was performing with the Houston stock company—but after seeing him in *Machinal,* she impulsively went backstage. He invited her to dinner.

Ria, 17 years Clark's senior, was born Maria Franklin. She had been married as a teenager to William Prentiss in Macomb, Illinois, but divorced him shortly after giving birth to a son. She then moved to Houston, where she married Alfred T. Lucas, an oil millionaire; they had two children. Upon Lucas' death she married the wealthy Andrew Langham. He died 12 years later.

Ria was small and shapely, and flashed beautiful brown eyes and auburn hair. Her fashion sense combined maximum taste with maximum glamor: she was always exceptionally well groomed. Ria was reputed to be a fascinating hostess, and, in her plush Park Avenue apartment, she loved to entertain friends in elegant style.

She was drawn to Clark, and he enjoyed her companionship, but their relationship was slow in developing. At first, it seemed unlikely that their friendship would turn into a romance. Clark was only in his late twenties; she was in her mid-forties. But she was wealth incarnate and he was a struggling actor! Lonely, insecure and discouraged, Gable accepted the much needed companionship and encouragement that Ria offered.

She welcomed him to her apartment and her parties, and she in-

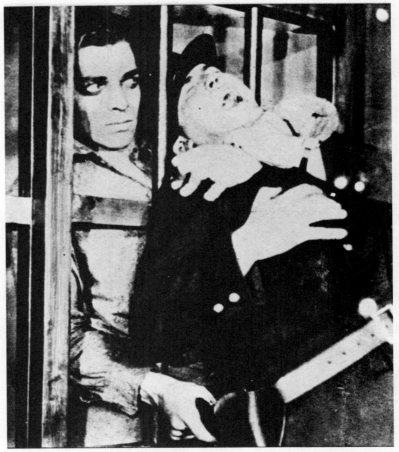

In 1930, Gable convincingly played "Killer" Mears in a Los Angeles stage production of The Last Mile.

troduced him to high society. This was Gable's first exposure to wealth, and through Ria, he learned quite a bit about good manners and proper dress.

Ria did something else for Clark. The two had been greatly impressed by Spencer Tracy playing Killer Mears in *The Last Mile* on the New York stage. Ria helped bring the drama to the West Coast in the summer of 1930. Not surprisingly, Clark was cast in the lead role. Playing a desperate criminal involved in a prison break, Gable was praised by critics for his vivid and forceful performance.

Now, back in California and earning $300 a week, Gable's acting began to attract the attention of Hollywood film studio casting directors. Lionel Barrymore was among those who had seen Clark in *The Last Mile*, and he arranged for Gable to be screen-tested by Metro-Goldwyn-Mayer (MGM). For the test, Clark's hair was curled and he was asked to wear a sarong and a hibiscus behind one ear (Barrymore was trying to get him a part in *Bird of Paradise*). In the test, Clark crept through bushes in search of a girl. Barrymore had emphasized to Clark that many screen actors couldn't speak well. But, strangely, Gable was given no lines in the test. And Barrymore, being away on location, was unable to coach the young aspirant.

Gable plays a scene in his first major talking film, The Painted Desert, *made late in 1930 and released early in 1931.*

Irving Thalberg of MGM looked at the film of the test and declared: "You can't put this man in a picture!"

Barrymore countered: "He's a good *stage* actor. He's young, but he'll be all right."

Thalberg snapped: "Not for my money, he won't. Look at his big, batlike ears."

Clark was not awarded the role in *Bird of Paradise.*

Shortly after this episode, in the summer of 1930, Gable was tested by Warner Brothers for the lead in *Little Caesar.* He was rejected by Darryl F. Zanuck, then head of production, who exclaimed, "His ears are too big!" Gable's hopes for a film career appeared shattered.

Miraculously, the despondent Clark received a call from Minna Wallis, an agent. She could get him a job playing a "heavy" in a western film, *The Painted Desert,* starring William Boyd and Helen Twelvetrees. All Gable had to do was ride a horse. Although he hadn't done any riding since boyhood days in Ohio, he quickly accepted the role. His salary was to be $750 a week. With five weeks to brush up on his horsemanship, Clark spent two hours daily taking riding lessons at a stable in the San Fernando Valley. By the time the film went on location, he was able to ride adequately.

When *The Painted Desert* was released in January, 1931, *Film Daily,* in its review, remarked: "He [Clark Gable] wasn't a very good cowboy, but the lady fans liked him. His brutish mannerisms were appropriate to the role."

Minna Wallis now placed Gable in a Warner Brothers production, *Night Nurse,* starring Barbara Stanwyck and Ben Lyon. He again portrayed a "heavy," this time a mean chauffeur who starves two children to death. *Night Nurse* was not released for a year, so Gable received no immediate feedback from the film.

Lionel Barrymore, who had been out of town during Gable's first MGM screen-test, arranged for a second test at MGM in the fall of 1930. This time, Barrymore took complete charge of the shooting. Gable was fitted with a dapper suit from wardrobe; a make-up man taped back his ears; and he was cautioned to keep his mouth closed because, despite dental work, his teeth were not particularly attractive.

This test was a big improvement, but no immediate decision was made. So Gable waited and pondered his future as an actor and even considered the possibility that he might do better on Broadway, despite his earlier disappointments there.

But within a few weeks, there was good news from agent Minna Wallis. She had contract offers for him from both RKO and MGM. Gable chose MGM. He was told that the studio had the finest writers, directors and technicians and he signed a six-month contract on December 4, 1930, at a salary of $350 per week.

Gable relaxes on the set early in his film career. He made a dozen pictures in his first year under contract with MGM.

Ria Langham (left), Gable's second wife, enjoys lunch with newspaper columnist Hedda Hopper.

Feeling secure in his new prosperity, Gable travelled to New York between film assignments. On March 29, 1931, in a quiet, unpublicized ceremony, he married Ria Langham. This was one day before Josephine's divorce would become final. For legal purposes, Clark remarried Ria in Santa Ana, California, in a private ceremony. An MGM publicity man was a witness.

Magazine and newspaper articles about Gable's personal life with Ria were sparse if for no other reason than that MGM's publicity department didn't think it would help Gable's career to play him up as a married man. A bachelor would have more box-office appeal, they reasoned.

Was Gable in love with Ria? Even Hollywood, famous for manufacturing love stories, never had much to say on the subject. Josephine Dillon later informed reporters: "Clark told me frankly that he wished to marry Ria Langham because she could do more for him financially."

Gable, 30 years of age at the time of his marriage, probably sought security in the 47-year-old Ria. The stability of a permanent home was something he had never known as a child—and he yearned for it.

In later years, Gable told an interviewer: "The older woman has seen more, heard more, and knows more than the demure little girl with a pretty face and shapely figure. I'll take the older woman every time."

Clark, no doubt, found what he sought in Ria. She was always at his side when he needed either a financial or emotional boost; he was now better dressed and better fed; he now even had the money to get his teeth capped.

Ria and Clark first settled in Ria's fashionable home in Beverly Hills. Later, they rented a luxurious six-room home at 220 North Bristol Street in Brentwood, a beautiful, wooded area of Los Angeles lying between Bel-Air and Santa Monica.

Gable's father, who had moved to California in 1931, lived with his son and daughter-in-law for a time—until the elder Gable married Edna, the widow of his brother Frank, at which time he moved to Hollywood.

During the 10 years since he left his oil field job, Clark and his father had had little contact. When success came to him in Hollywood, Clark decided to get in touch with him again.

Clark had become increasingly interested in hunting, fishing, camping and skeetshooting. One of his favorite fishing spots was "Rainbow" Gibson's We Ask U Inn, a lodge on the Rogue River in Oregon. Another favorite was a Bakersfield, California skeet club owned by Harry and Nan Fleischmann of the Fleischmann's Yeast family. Ria, who preferred high society life and entertaining friends at home, accompanied him on his outdoor trips—but only as a spectator.

Gable's first MGM role was a minor one. He played a laundryman in *The Easiest Way* (released in 1931), starring Constance Bennett, Adolphe Menjou, Robert Montgomery and Anita Page. But MGM soon cast him with Joan Crawford in *Dance, Fools, Dance,* the second of a dozen pictures Gable was to make for MGM in 1931. *Variety* appraised his portrayal of a gangster as a "vivid and authentic piece of acting."

In his next picture, *The Secret Six,* starring Wallace Beery, Lewis Stone, John Mack Brown and Jean Harlow, Gable played a reporter assigned to investigate gangland killings. *The New York Times* described his acting as "forceful." He followed this with another gangster role, that of mob leader Louis Blanco in *The Finger Points,* starring Richard Barthelmess, Fay Wray and Regis Toomey. "Clark Gable again scores with his fine voice and magnetic personality," commented *Film Daily.*

Gable was teamed with Joan Crawford again, this time in *Laughing Sinners.* He played a Salvation Army worker. *The New York Times* wrote: "New leading man Clark Gable is rather unconvincing as the saviour of fallen Crawford, who is better than usual in a film that is less than average in its overall scheme."

His next picture, *A Free Soul,* was to prove very significant. It helped forge the Gable image that was to endure for years. In this film, he played a gambler and underworld leader who slaps Norma Shearer, the picture's star, who in real life was the wife of the producer, Irving Thalberg. When the picture was released, moviegoers saw an actor who could be "naughty" but "nice." Cascades of favorable Clark Gable fan mail poured in. Some women confessed: "I would *love* to be slapped by that man."

It was 1931. Rudolph Valentino had been dead for five years and handsome actor John Gilbert's squeaky voice led him to become a casualty of the "talky" era. The public was ready for a new kind of rugged he-man male star. Gable was the man they chose.

Gable makes love to Norma Shearer in A Free Soul, *a 1931 film in which Gable also slapped Norma's face.*

Following *A Free Soul,* which had helped establish his image, *Night Nurse,* made in 1930, was finally released in August of 1931. Gable played the rough chauffeur who punches a lot of people, including Barbara Stanwyck. Next, he was cast in the leading role of a gambler opposite Madge Evans in *Sporting Blood.* Moving up to star status, he was assigned the lead opposite Greta Garbo in *Susan Lennox: Her Fall and Rise and Fall.* Garbo, already a big star, overshadowed Gable in the film, but Clark, playing a construction engineer, received generally favorable reviews.

In that very first year at MGM, Gable quickly commanded attention. Hailed as one of the most exciting performers to come along in years, MGM female stars, studio workers, the press, and the public enthusiastically applauded Gable and his fan mail increased.

Madge Evans was Gable's co-star in Sporting Blood, *a 1931 picture in which Clark played a gambler.*

Greta Garbo and Gable made love in Susan Lennox—Her Fall and Rise and Fall, *another 1931 film.*

Gable, at age 30, in 1931. The short hair style failed to hide his big ears that became a famous trademark.

An article in the July 13, 1931 issue of *The Hollywood Reporter* said of Gable: "A *star* is in the making. Has been made. A star that, to our reckoning, will outdraw every other star. ... Never have we seen audiences work themselves into such enthusiasm as when Gable walks on the screen."

Several months later, syndicated newspaper columnist Harry Carr wrote: "Every time Gable appears on the screen, an electric shock runs through all female hearts for miles around. Women are mad about him."

Gable particularly enjoyed the sudden attention because his sex appeal had gone relatively unnoticed on Broadway. He decided to celebrate his new-found fame and income; he bought a used Duesenberg, of which he was extremely proud. Always fond of automobiles, Gable often said: "If when I was a kid some rich man who owned a car that fascinated me had hired me as his chauffeur, I think I would have been happy for the rest of my life—driving it and keeping it in shape." Now, he no longer had to fantasize; he had an automobile of his own.

Gable was then cast once again with Joan Crawford in the film *Possessed,* which was released in 1931. He played a wealthy young lawyer. *Film Daily's* review said Gable "has come a long way from his villain roles. His performance suggests that he may become a solid actor."

Villain roles may have helped Gable in his rise to stardom. "The new actor has a much better chance of being recognized in the role of a villain than as the leading man," Gable later explained. "The villain does things that are outside the range of normal human conduct and is therefore memorable."

In 1931, while filming *Possessed,* in a role which called for him to be madly in love with Crawford, Clark began seeing his leading lady after hours. The youthful, beautiful star was having marital problems with her husband, Douglas Fairbanks, Jr. Rumors were rampant: "What star is interested in her leading man?" Meanwhile, Clark and Joan went for quiet rides by the sea. They talked of marriage, but she didn't want to hurt Ria, whom she admired. Crawford later revealed that she doubted that their romance could last, and she chose to settle for friendship.

Clark next portrayed a Naval Air Force petty officer, a rival of Wallace Beery. Most of this film, *Hell Divers,* consisted of flying scenes; there was very little love interest provided by Gable and Dorothy Jordon.

As a result of the 12 films in which Gable acted in 1931, he was dubbed "Valentino in Jack Dempsey's body," and went from a virtually unknown stage actor to become a major screen star.

An MGM publicity man, Howard Strickling, did much to publicize Gable during this period of his career, and he was very careful in selecting what information he would feed to the public. Strickling handled many personal details for the new star, and the two became good friends.

Gable's contract was rewritten in December, 1931, and his salary was

(Above and top right) Gable, in 1932, at age 31, revealed a handsome profile, with or without a mustache.

increased to $1,150 a week for a one-year period. This was considered a fantastic increase, although still not in keeping with what the big stars were earning. Gable might have bargained for more, but the Great Depression had set in and money was tight.

The 1930s became known as the "Golden Age" of the motion picture industry, a time when giant film studios were fat with talent. Gable was fortunate to be signed with MGM, the biggest, richest and most productive of all studios. Ruled by Louis B. Mayer, MGM was associated with the extensive Loew's theater chain, and had access to the largest film outlet in the world.

After his dozen pictures in 1931, Gable's next was a mistake. He was miscast as Reverend John Hartley in *Polly of the Circus*. The film, also starring Marion Davies, was released in 1932. It did nothing to enhance his image.

But Gable's next film, *Red Dust,* also a 1932 release, saw him cast in a role more true to his image: the boss of a rubber plantation in a remote area of Indo-China, who encounters a prostitute on the run. The prostitute was played by a sultry platinum blonde sex queen, Jean Harlow. The film featured a famous scene wherein Gable helps Harlow bathe in a rain barrel. Critics gave both Gable and Harlow very good reviews.

(Left) The angle at which this January, 1933 photograph was taken drew attention to Gable's large ears. (Below) This 1932 bathing scene from Red Dust, featuring sexy platinum blonde Jean Harlow, received considerable publicity.

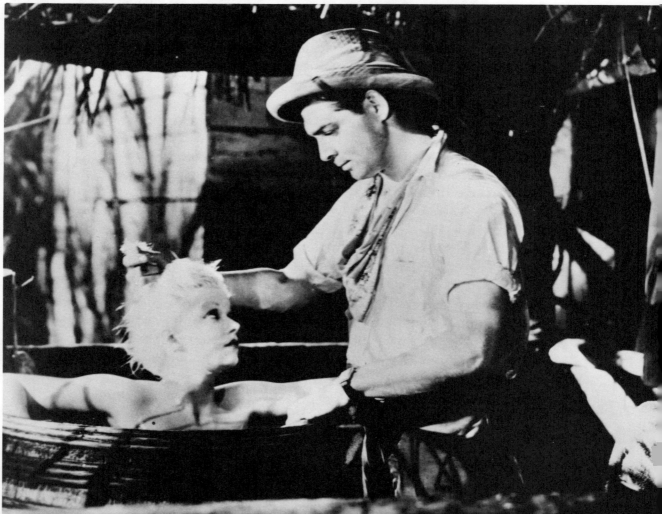

After making *Strange Interlude* with Norma Shearer, Gable was "loaned" to Paramount Studios to play opposite Carole Lombard, the lovely blonde comedienne, in *No Man of Her Own,* released on December 31, 1932. He portrayed a big-time card shark who married the town beauty on a bet, only to fall in love with her later. The picture was strong on romance, drama and comedy. Both *Strange Interlude* and *No Man of Her Own* were lauded, along with the stars.

After appearing twice with Helen Hayes in *The White Sister* and *Night Flight,* and again with Jean Harlow in *Hold Your Man*—all 1933 releases—Gable was cast as a stage director in *Dancing Lady.* It co-starred Joan Crawford and Franchot Tone.

Gable, now earning $2,500 a week, complained to MGM. He disliked his role in the film. Moreover, he disliked the picture. MGM officials were irked. They believed Gable was avoiding shooting the film by scheduling both an appendectomy *and* a tonsilectomy. The operations sidelined the actor for a couple of months. In truth, the long hours and hard work that Gable had put in for several years had affected his health. He had already lost much weight and was concerned about his well-being.

MGM decided to "lend" Gable to Columbia Studios in 1934. The star was upset. He later told reporters: "At that time Columbia was on the wrong side of the tracks, and being sent there was a 'this-will-teach-you-a-lesson deal'. . . . I felt that I had just been swept out of MGM's executive offices with the morning's trash."

Although at home with comedy on the stage, Gable had up to this point had little experience with it on the screen. He was flabbergasted to find himself immediately cast opposite Claudette Colbert in Columbia's production of *It Happened One Night.* "You've got a fine script," he told Frank Capra, the director. "Why you've chosen me to be in it, *I* don't know. You've never seen me play comedy on the screen." Gable also informed Capra: "If you think I can do it, I'll try, but after three or four days, if you don't like what you see on the screen, you can call the whole thing off and there'll be no hard feelings."

The picture was a great success. Gable played a newspaper reporter who has just been fired from his job and meets an heiress (Claudette Colbert) traveling incognito. The movie contains several memorable situations. Audiences particularly liked the hitchhiking scene in which Claudette lifts her skirt and shows her leg to stop a car. In another favorite moment, Clark places a hanging blanket between them when they sleep in the same hotel room. The picture, scheduled to run a week, ran a month and won Academy Awards for Gable and Colbert as Best Actor and Best Actress. It was named Best Picture of 1934, won Best Director Award for Capra, and Best Adaptation for Robert Riskin, the screenwriter.

In the film, Gable at one point removed his shirt to reveal that he was not wearing an undershirt. This resulted in considerable publicity and a decline in undershirt sales. (Gable later admitted that he hadn't worn an undershirt since youth.)

It Happened One Night hurled Gable into major stardom. MGM hiked his salary to over $200,000 a year; only a handful of stars were making more. On a cross-country trip to New York with Ria, Gable was mobbed by female fans at every train stop.

Gable, as a slick confidence man, made love to Jean Harlow in the 1933 film, Hold Your Man.

(Right) Gable was called "The Screen's Great Lover" in this 1933 newspaper advertisement for No Man of Her Own, *the only film he ever made with Carole Lombard.*

(Below) Sales of men's undershirts declined when Gable revealed that he wasn't wearing one in this scene from It Happened One Night, *co-starring Claudette Colbert.*

(Right) Gable is about to kiss Myrna Loy in Men in White. *In the 1934 film, Clark played a struggling doctor, Myrna played the daughter of a wealthy man.*

(Left) Gable, as a reporter, and Claudette Colbert, as a runaway heiress, in the famous hitchhiking scene from It Happened One Night.

Like Rudolph Valentino, his physical presence always caused excitement—even in Hollywood, where people were "immune" to movie stars. Of course, hundreds of fans waited daily at the MGM studio gates yearning for just a glimpse of their idol. There was a mystique about Gable that involved more than just his tall, dark and handsome physique that caused both men and women to turn around and take a second look.

When Gable accepted his Oscar on February 27, 1935, he was stunned. All he could say was "thank you." At age 34, he had finally achieved the fame and fortune that had eluded him for nearly 17 years, and he found himself practically speechless.

Reports began to emerge that Gable's marriage to Ria was in trouble. Word had it that, like Josephine Dillon, Ria was mothering him, ordering him around. She spent much time and money throwing lavish, formal dinner parties and demanded that Clark take care of details, such as flowers or instructions to the butler. Ria was extravagant; Clark was frugal, never having forgotten his childhood poverty.

The convincing love scenes between Gable and Loretta Young in Call of the Wild *sparked rumors of an off-screen affair.*

Gable poses with Movita, his love interest in Mutiny On the Bounty, *on the island of Tahiti.*

She enjoyed entertaining Hollywood's most influential people: the Samuel Goldwyns; Irving Thalberg and his wife, Norma Shearer; Gloria Swanson; Helen Hayes; Joan Crawford; Mary Pickford; Marlene Dietrich; Joseph Schenck; and David O. Selznick and his wife, Irene Mayer Selznick, daughter of Louis B. Mayer. Gable did not enjoy partying.

Whereas Ria relished high society life, Clark longed for the outdoors. He felt more comfortable in sport clothes than dress clothes. MGM officials had urged him to pursue hunting and other outdoor sports to further his image as a he-man. Gable did so—but only because he enjoyed these activities.

Gable's appearances with Joan Crawford in the 1933 film, *Dancing Lady,* and in a 1934 release, *Forsaking All Others,* again sparked whispers of romance. Rumors of Gable's involvement in other extramarital affairs surfaced as well. Fan magazines and newspaper gossip columns reported that he was dating starlets and Broadway showgirls. In 1935, there was talk of a love affair between Gable and Loretta Young, his beautiful co-star in *Call of the Wild.* The picture, shot on location, kept them in an isolated area near Mount Baker, Washington, for nearly three months.

Gable played a courageous seaman in Mutiny On the Bounty, *which received the Academy Award for Best Picture in 1935.*

Rumors continued, and later in 1935 Gable was cast in what turned out to be one of his most important films, *Mutiny on the Bounty,* with Charles Laughton. At first, he did not relish the role. "I thought *Mutiny on the Bounty* was not for me," he explained, "because all the cast, except Franchot Tone, was English. I felt that playing an Englishman among Englishmen was a little too much. I didn't like the idea of wearing knee breeches. But I did it anyway."

Mutiny on the Bounty won the Academy Award for Best Picture of 1935, and Gable was highly praised for his characterization of Fletcher Christian, challenger to the sadistic Captain Bligh (Charles Laughton) on the South Seas.

Meanwhile, matrimonial seas were getting still rougher for Gable. He separated from Ria, went on a 10-week combination holiday/promotional tour of South America, and when he returned in November, 1935, moved into the Beverly Wilshire Hotel. "Mrs. Gable is a fine woman, and whatever fault there is, blame it on me," Gable told reporters. Ria said that the deterioration of the marriage was due to the constant pressure to which her husband was subjected, his sudden success, and the adulation

The happy couple, Ria and Clark, separated after only five years of marriage. They were legally divorced in 1939.

of his female fans. She did not discuss the difference in their ages. He was now nearly 35, she was approaching 52.

Gable did not file for divorce. He felt it unwise financially, for California's community property law stipulated that a wife be awarded one-half of the couple's assets. The separation agreement he had arranged with Ria was already costing him $2,000 per week—half of his salary. That was all he wanted to pay.

Although still legally married, Gable now openly dated other women. No longer the insecure, impoverished youngster he once was, Hollywood speculated that perhaps the mature Gable's next move was to find love with a younger woman. This would be truer to the image the star projected on the screen.

3
In Love with Carole

ON JANUARY 25, 1936, HAVING been separated from Ria for two months, Clark Gable decided to attend a ball called The White Mayfair. The extravagant affair, sponsored by the Mayfair Club as a benefit for the Motion Picture Relief Fund, was typical of Hollywood parties of the 1930s. It was a formal event, requiring men to be dressed in white tie and tails, and women in white gowns. Six footmen in white jackets and red satin knee breeches were hired to attend to the arriving guests.

More than 300 people—most of them film stars or studio executives—were expected. It was to be a "Who's Who" of Hollywood. Gloria Swanson, Janet Gaynor, Merle Oberon, Spencer Tracy, Harold Lloyd, Bing Crosby, Douglas Fairbanks, Irene Dunne, Fredric March, Dolores Del Rio, Jeanette MacDonald, Humphrey Bogart, Barbara Stanwyck, Basil Rathbone, Alice Faye, Loretta Young, Buster Keaton, James Stewart, Claudette Colbert, Marion Davies, David Niven and Henry Fonda would all be present. So, too, would film industry moguls Darryl F. Zanuck, Adolph Zukor, Jack L. Warner, Ernst Lubitsch, Louis B. Mayer and Harry Cohn.

Many glamorous ladies attended The White Mayfair, which was held at the plush Victor Hugo's restaurant in Beverly Hills. As Gable mingled among the crowd that evening, with the music of Cab Calloway and Eduardo Durantes playing in the background, one particular woman caught his attention. That woman was Carole Lombard, a blue-eyed, golden-haired beauty. It was common knowledge that Carole, who served as the party's hostess, had been escorted to the event by Cesar Romero. Miss Lombard, a chain-smoking, talkative girl who used swear words freely, was visibly outraged because Norma Shearer was wearing a bright

Carole Lombard, Hollywood's most famous comedienne in the thirties, became Gable's No. 1 love interest in 1936.

crimson gown. The invitations had stipulated that women wear *white*. Carole, although the hostess, could not bar Norma Shearer from the party. Norma was, after all, Mrs. Irving Thalberg in private life, and Thalberg was one of Hollywood's most important figures.

Clark approached Carole. He quietly uttered: "I go for you, Ma." She immediately recognized the nickname he had given her during the filming of *No Man of Her Own.* She smiled as he asked her to dance. "I go for you, too, Pa," she said, using the name she had given him during the film.

It had been four years since Lombard and Gable had seen each other. During the making of the 1932 picture they had shared nothing more than a friendship. She was then married to William Powell; Clark was married to Ria.

Now, on this January night in 1936, they were a beautiful couple on the dance floor. Clark had actually become more handsome than she had remembered him. His broad shoulders filled out the tuxedo which had been neatly fitted on his six-foot, 195-pound, "no-waist, no-hip" physique. Carole, a petite woman of five-feet-two, 112 pounds, and with a good figure, looked ravishing in her form-fitting white gown. She was a mere 27 years old, nearly half the age of Ria, who was somewhere in the crowd. Clark held Carole closely; she felt good in his arms. He looked at her with his light grey eyes that darted out from his dark face, and he flashed his famous enigmatic smile. Surely, Carole would be attracted to his strong animal magnetism.

Later in the evening, Clark asked Carole to leave the party and go for a ride with him in his Duesenberg. She accepted. After riding for awhile, he stopped at the Beverly Wilshire Hotel and invited her up to his apartment for a drink.

"Who do you think you are, *Clark Gable?*" quipped Carole. Clark saw nothing funny in the remark. He abruptly drove away from the hotel and, at high speed, returned to the Mayfair Ball.

Later that evening, Clark again asked Carole to leave the party with him. She declined, explaining that after the ball she would be hosting a breakfast party at home for some friends. Shortly after midnight, she invited Clark to join her at her Hollywood home and to help prepare for the guests. Clark accepted, but soon found out that she had hoped he would serve as bartender.

When he realized her motive, he left her before any guests had arrived, explaining that he had another appointment.

"With who, *Loretta Young?*" quipped Carole.

This angered Clark. Dejected, he returned to his hotel.

Gable awakened the next morning at the Beverly Wilshire to find two doves in his hotel room. They had been delivered in a gilded cage—a gift from Carole. She included a note: "How about it?"

Encouraged by the message and gift, he immediately phoned her,

Blonde-haired, blue-eyed Carole Lombard had winged eyebrows, a style which was widely copied by the women of the thirties.

apologized for his behavior, and asked for a date. But she refused, saying she was busy. Clark called again and again, but each time Carole said that she was still too busy.

It was two weeks later, on February 7, at the home of millionaire John Hay Whitney, before the two met again. Gable and MGM screenwriter Donald Ogden Stewart planned a party to cheer up Stewart's wife who was recuperating from a nervous breakdown. The party was set for noon. Everyone was urged to "dress" for the event, which was dubbed "Bea Stewart's Annual Nervous Breakdown Party." As Gable welcomed guests at the Whitney mansion, he heard the wailing sound of an ambulance

Gable is shown with the Model T Ford that Carole Lombard bought him as a Valentine's Day "gift" in 1936.

siren. He opened the door as the vehicle pulled to a quick halt. Two uniformed attendants, carrying a stretcher bearing a figure under a white sheet walked to the door and, ignoring the puzzled onlookers—including Wallace Beery and Robert Taylor—proceeded to the living room and set down the stretcher. Under the sheet, her face barely showing and her eyes closed, lay Carole Lombard. The partygoers were stunned. Had she been in an accident? Carole suddenly sat upright and burst into an hysterical fit of laughter. No one else was amused.

"What's the matter with everyone? Can't you tell a gag when you see one?" she snapped, adding a few choice cuss words. Gable was displeased with the joke and took Carole aside to tell her so.

The party proceeded as planned and Gable and Lombard spent most of the afternoon playing tennis on the Whitney courts. Carole won every set. She rewarded her opponent with a kiss for being such a good loser.

Clark and Carole made a date for Valentine's Day. On the morning of that day, a beat-up Model T Ford was delivered to Gable at the MGM lot. Carole had purchased it for $15 at a local junk yard. The car was barely in running condition: the exterior was dented and scratched; the interior upholstery was moldy and shredded. Some of the springs were exposed, and the fenders were badly bent and cracked. The Model T was painted white —with big red hearts. It was a unique Valentine's Day gift, indeed!

Gable *loved* it. He decided to play along with the gag. That night, after having some quick engine repair work done, he took Carole for a drive in the car. She, dressed in a beautiful gown and wrapped in a white chinchilla jacket, sat at Clark's side as the Model T chugged, jerked and wheezed down the Hollywood thoroughfares to the famous, plush Trocadero night club.

Hollywood started buzzing about the budding Gable-Lombard romance; it could be the love story of the decade. This real-life romance was very much like a film scenario: a handsome actor who is unhappily married falls in love with a beautiful blonde girl who is witty and winsome.

It was 1936. Carole Lombard was well known to the public for her beauty and her comedy film roles. She had reached stardom much sooner than Gable. Under contract to Paramount Pictures for six years, she was earning $3,000 per week, making her one of the studio's leading female stars along with Claudette Colbert, Marlene Dietrich and Mae West.

Carole was well liked in the film colony; she was known for a gaiety that bubbled like champagne. At parties or in night clubs, her table was invariably the noisiest and wittiest. She was restless, high-strung, loved people and was exceedingly talkative. She spoke fast, but was a good listener as well. She didn't want to miss a word, and when she listened, she did it with a brisk, "Yah, yah, I get you," or "That's right." And if she agreed, she used one of her favorite expressions: "It's O.K. by me." She traveled from her busy dressing room (where there was always commotion, music, and ringing phones) to stages on the movie lot in a motor scooter. She waved and smiled at all who passed. Her vitality was endless. This was the Carole Lombard of 1936. Her background is interesting:

Born Jane Alice Peters on October 6, 1908, in Fort Wayne, Indiana, she had a melting pot heritage; her ancestors were Scotch, Irish, Welsh and German. Carole's grandfather, John Peters, was the man who carried America's first washing machine all the way from Germany. He founded Horton Manufacturing Company in Fort Wayne. Her father later became a Horton executive, and was a wealthy man.

When Jane was seven, her parents separated. She went to California with her mother and two brothers. They intended to stay for six months, but the family liked California and decided to remain indefinitely.

Jane was placed in a private school. She later took a three-year course at a dramatics school where she appeared in several dramatic productions. Concurrently, she appeared in stage plays in Los Angeles area theaters. In school, Jane enjoyed athletics—soccer, tennis, sprints and broad jumping —more than her studies. A true tomboy, she played first base with neighborhood ball teams organized by her brother.

While still in her teens, Jane began playing bit parts in motion pictures during summer vacations. An auto accident in 1925 nearly ended her movie career. She had gone for a drive with a friend and the brakes locked suddenly. She was thrown through the windshield and her face was badly lacerated. Rushed to a hospital, Jane underwent surgery without anesthetic—lest her facial muscles relax and render the surgery useless. She was told to keep her facial muscles immobile for 10 days. She made a good recovery and was not permanently scarred.

When the wounds had healed, Jane obtained work in Mack Sennett comedies, exchanging custard pies with Buster Keaton and others in the wild-eyed troupe. After a year and a half in the Sennett comedies, she landed a role at Fox Studios in *Me, Gangster.* She did well enough to win a contract with Pathe.

While at Pathe, where she was earning $150 a week, Jane was summoned to the office of studio head Joseph P. Kennedy, President Kennedy's father. Kennedy told her she was too fat. She weighed 121 pounds at the time, and she agreed to undergo reducing treatments. However, before leaving his office, she informed Kennedy: "You're not so skinny yourself." With that Jane strutted out of the office, slamming the door behind her. Jane lost 10 pounds, never to have a weight problem again. She always kept her figure at a trim 112 pounds.

Jane Alice Peters became known as Carole Lombard and landed a contract with Paramount. Madalynne Fields (nicknamed "Fieldsie"), who had acted as a comic in Mack Sennett films, was hired as Carole's full-time secretary and business adviser. Fieldsie helped negotiate the Paramount contract. Paramount, which had become one of Hollywood's biggest studios, enrolled Carole in dramatic, dancing and singing classes as part of a training program for new contract players.

No actress in Hollywood was more popular with the film crews than the young Carole Lombard. She was loved by everyone on the set—electricians, cameramen, hairdressers, make-up artists, and studio police. She was an inveterate joker; all were enchanted by her.

Carole had not always been a free-talker, and confident. During her early years in pictures, she was tense and nervous before the cameras. When she examined her work, she realized that she wasn't a very good actress, and that she would have to rely on personality. So, she decided to create an image for herself. By being noisy, and giving the appearance of being happy-go-lucky and gay, people started to notice her. Gradually, she gained confidence and through this confidence became a better actress.

Lombard's rise as an actress began in 1931 when she appeared with William Powell in *Man of the World,* a Paramount release. She had met Powell—16 years older than she, and a sophisticated ladies' man—in the fall of 1930. They were married eight months later. Their marriage lasted a little over two years.

In 1934, shortly after her divorce from Powell had become legal, she was frequently seen in the company of Russ Columbo, a dark-haired, handsome, young radio and screen singer. He was proving to be more popular than Rudy Vallee and was giving a new singer, Bing Crosby, good competition. Carole tried to help Columbo, who bore a striking resemblance to Rudolph Valentino, get some movie roles.

Hollywood gossip columnists wrote much about the Lombard-Columbo romance. But, although the couple had been seeing each other regularly for nearly a year, and there was talk of marriage, both continued to deny any engagement. They were only good friends, they claimed.

On August 31, 1934, after attending a preview of Columbo's latest film, Carole went to Lake Arrowhead to spend the Labor Day weekend. She was accompanied only by her secretary. On Sunday night, her mother phoned with the shocking news that Columbo had been accidentally shot by an old Civil War ball and cap pistol. He and Lansing V. Brown, Jr., a Hollywood photographer, were examining the weapon in the trophy room of Brown's home. The bullet first struck the top of a mahogany table, then hit Columbo in the eye and embedded itself in his brain; the wound was fatal. The nation was shocked by the news. Columbo was dead at the age of 26 and Carole went into mourning. "His love for me was the kind that rarely comes to any woman," she told reporters.

In 1936, when Carole met Gable, she had been spending time with screenwriter Robert Riskin, who had worked on *It Happened One Night*. He had become her most constant companion after Columbo's death. Lombard and Riskin were not romantically involved; theirs was a platonic relationship. Carole remained romantically uninvolved.

The Gable-Lombard romance did not develop smoothly. Clark had difficulty reaching a property settlement with Ria, and he knew that he could not enter into another marriage until he and Ria could agree on divorce terms.

Carole, on the other hand, had to determine whether she was falling in love with the Clark Gable of the *screen* or the *real* Clark Gable. Off-screen, she found that Gable was a quiet, shy man who sometimes appeared lonely and sad. This confused her. In addition, she was still recovering from her divorce from Powell and from Columbo's death, and she wanted to be sure that Clark really loved her and was not using her to further his own career.

Throughout 1936, Gable and Lombard dated each other frequently. They sometimes dined at Hollywood's famous Brown Derby, or enjoyed a quiet dinner at Carole's home. They often dressed informally and ate at out-of-the-way places where they could be as inconspicuous as possible. They were afforded little privacy when they went to Hollywood movie premieres, the Trocadero or the Ambassador Hotel's Coconut Grove; press photographers always awaited their appearance. So they spent much time alone. The couple enjoyed horseback riding. When they didn't mind being in the company of others, they often attended boxing, wrestling or tennis matches.

Marriage was mentioned, but Clark tabled any discussion. He was unable to meet Ria's financial demands for a divorce settlement, and until such a settlement was reached, it was pointless to discuss marriage with Carole. Rumors of Ria boasting that Clark was begging her not to file a divorce were widespread. There was also talk that Gable enjoyed his status as a legally separated man, free to see other women.

The rumors probably didn't bother Carole much for she knew the ways of film colony gossip. She did, however, become irritated when, on one occasion, she read a magazine article in which Gable was quoted as saying that he would probably never remarry because a wife of his would be unable to tolerate the many women who chased him. It led to a brief argument, but Gable and Lombard soon made up.

Carole often had roses sent to Gable when he was working at MGM. On this particular occasion in 1938, photographed here, Carole made the delivery personally.

When Gable's work kept him too busy to conduct a full social life with Carole, she occasionally dated other men. A legendary story about one of Carole's dates tells of the time when Anthony Quinn, then not yet a star, was supposed to take her out but didn't show up. When Carole next saw him, she scorched his ears with an abundance of swear words, calming down only when she learned that Quinn did not show up because he could not *afford* to take her out. His income as a struggling actor was just above subsistence. As a result, she helped Quinn further his career by contacting an agent and talking to film directors in his behalf.

Gable's film career was moving at a rapid pace. He received good reviews for his 1936 picture, *San Francisco,* about the great 1906 earthquake, in which he played the ruthless proprietor of the infamous Paradise Cafe. Spencer Tracy co-starred as an understanding priest. In the same year, Lombard starred with William Powell in *My Man Godfrey,* a "screwball" comedy picture that earned Lombard an Academy Award nomina-

Gable, Jack Holt, Spencer Tracy (as a priest) and Jeanette MacDonald in a scene from San Francisco in 1936.

Gable and Wallace Beery, his co-star in China Seas, *hold a discussion with Irving Thalberg of MGM, who died in 1936.*

tion. The success of the film also sparked a $150,000-per-picture contract with Paramount. The contract granted her special privileges: the right to choose her own cameraman, and approval of the selection of the director and supporting cast.

Later in 1936, Gable made *Love on the Run* with Joan Crawford. Lombard had no need to worry about a romance rekindling between Clark and Joan. Crawford was now married to Franchot Tone, who was also appearing in the picture. She played an heiress, and Gable a reporter, the plot being a take-off on *It Happened One Night*.

Gable began 1937 with some good news and publicity. He was chosen to place his foot and handprints in cement on the forecourt of Grauman's Chinese Theater. This was one of the greatest honors Hollywood had to offer, the mark of having achieved full-fledged stardom. Gable's appearance drew the largest crowd since Grauman originated the print idea 10 years earlier.

Gable's next picture was a fiasco. He was terribly miscast as a poetic Irish Patriot in *Parnell.* The movie got poor reviews and suffered a financial loss.

While filming *Parnell,* Judy Garland, then a 13-year-old singer, sang "You Made Me Love You" at Clark's 36th birthday party. Special lyrics had been written for the occasion. The song began: "Dear Mr. Gable, I am writing this to you, and I hope that you will read it so you'll know my heart beats like a hammer and I stutter and I stammer everytime I see you at the picture show. I guess I'm just another fan of yours, and I thought I'd write and tell you so. You made me love you, I didn't want to do it, I didn't want to do it. . . ." Gable was impressed. He grabbed Judy in his arms and kissed her on the cheek, whispering, "Thanks, honey, that was a real thrill." (Judy later recorded the song and sang it in *Broadway Melody of 1938.)*

The year 1937 brought some bad news for Gable as well. Newspapers carried the story about an Englishwoman, Mrs. Violet Wells Norton, who charged that Gable had fathered her 13-year-old daughter, Gwendolyn. Norton declared that Gable had been in England in 1922 and 1923 under

Gable was terribly miscast as an Irish patriot in Parnell, *a 1937 release that received many bad reviews.*

Carole and Clark are seen enjoying the horse races at Hollywood Park in 1938.

the name of Frank Billings. She said that when she later saw Gable in one of his pictures, "there was Frank Billings (Gable) on the screen." She wrote to Gable about the claim, but he discarded the letter. Mrs. Norton persisted, demanding $100,000 against the threat of public exposure. MGM had the case brought to trial. Gable had a star witness—his former girl friend, Franz Doerfler—testify in his behalf. She swore that she was with Clark in the fall of 1922 when the baby was allegedly conceived in England.

A surprise witness was Harry Billings, brother of the phantom Frank Billings. He testified that Clark was *not* his brother. Another key witness was a representative of the Passport Office who testified that no passport had been issued to Gable to enable him to leave or re-enter the country in 1922. Gable easily won the case and Mrs. Norton, indicted for using the mails to defraud, was found guilty and sentenced to one year in jail.

Several months after the conclusion of the trial, something happened which would greatly affect Gable: Jean Harlow, who co-starred with him for the sixth time in *Saratoga,* became seriously ill before the picture was completed. She died of uremic poisoning, following acute infection of the gall bladder and damaging of her kidneys. The death of the sex symbol of the 1930s shocked Gable and the nation. She was young (26) and beautiful, and death had come suddenly.

MGM's switchboards were swamped with calls inquiring about the actual cause of Harlow's death. Rumors ran rampant. Some suspected that heavy drinking had ruined her; others that she had died as a result of an abortion; still others that she had been beaten to death by her second husband, Paul Bern.

Although Gable was not romantically linked with Harlow, he had grown quite fond of her through the years and their six pictures together. He called her "Sis," although most people around the studio referred to her as "The Baby."

On June 9, 1937, Gable served as a pallbearer and usher at Jean's funeral. *Saratoga,* just a week away from completion at the time of her death, was finished by using Harlow's double, Mary Dees, in long camera shots (many without her face to the camera).

Saratoga was rushed into an early release. It opened on July 23, 1937, only six weeks after Harlow's funeral. The picture was a huge box office success. Gable's career, which had faltered after *Parnell,* soared once again.

4
Gone with the Wind

IN 1937 AND 1938 CLARK AND CAROLE had very busy schedules. They sometimes worked 10 hours a day, six days a week, and had little time to enjoy each other. Exhausted at the end of the work day, Carole often went to sleep as early as 8:30 p.m.

Gable had learned that his legal wife, Ria, had hired private detectives to trail him, so he continued to maintain his Beverly Wilshire Hotel room for "appearance" only. Clark and Carole agreed to see each other less in public so as not to irritate Ria, who was becoming more excessive in her settlement demands. An eight-page feature article in *Look* magazine, "The Love Story of Clark Gable and Carole Lombard," resulted in Ria demanding an increase in weekly payments.

A two-page article in *Photoplay* entitled, "Can the Gable-Lombard Love Story Have a Happy Ending?" reported that "his love for Ria is dying, if it be not dead." The article added that the Gable-Lombard romance was being written by time—and "time will furnish its climax and its end. It may be one of the deepest tragedies, one of the most poignant romances of Hollywood. . . . How will the drama end? Will one of the lovers forsake the other? Will they both, someday, regard the cold ashes of their love, and sigh a little? Or, will they wait, patiently, chins up, brave smiles painted on their faces, never flagging in their romance?"

It became increasingly obvious that Gable loved Lombard. But, despite this, Gable was slow in obtaining a divorce from Ria. He had refused to make the financial sacrifice and it was not easy for Carole to understand Gable's frugality. She was a free spender, quick to help studio workers in financial difficulty, and liberal in her dispensation of monies to charities. Despite their differences, Gable and Lombard were in love, and they spent as much time together as possible.

"Wherever Clark and Carole were, people collected instinctively," wrote Hedda Hopper, the syndicated Hollywood columnist. "At the Trocadero, after the premiere of *Marie Antoinette,* there was a party for MGM's Norma Shearer, then queen of the MGM lot, but Clark and Carole got all the attention. Big stars and producers crowded around the center table where they sat."

Seeking more privacy for himself and Carole, Clark rented a small house in secluded Laurel Canyon. When Ria learned about it, Gable gave it up, moved out of the Beverly Wilshire Hotel, and leased a home in North Hollywood which formerly belonged to director Rex Ingram and his wife, actress Alice Terry. Gable figured Ria couldn't object to that; he had to have a place to live. Nevertheless, Carole had to be careful about the amount of time she spent there.

Gable's relationship with Lombard seemed to be strengthening his character. Friends and acquaintances noticed that he had become more self-confident and aggressive since meeting Carole.

Carole had changed considerably, too. Once a lover of big parties, nightclubs and people, she now seemed content to be alone with Clark, and became more and more interested in the things he enjoyed. One of his favorite pastimes was skeetshooting, and Gable taught her how to fire a 20-gauge Winchester rifle. She also learned how to fly-cast so she could go fishing. The movie star couple might also be found duck hunting near Bakersfield, at a private gun club to which Gable belonged.

After *Saratoga,* released in 1937, Gable went to work on *Test Pilot,* playing the title role of a pilot who falls in love with a woman (Myrna Loy) on whose farm he has made a forced landing. Spencer Tracy was cast as his mechanic and Lionel Barrymore as his employer.

While still working on the film Gable received a major boost: Ed Sullivan, a movie columnist for the *Chicago Tribune-New York Daily News* syndicate, conducted a contest in 400 newspapers throughout the United States in which more than 20 million voters were to name their choices for the "King" and "Queen" of Hollywood. Gable was officially crowned "King"; Myrna Loy was named "Queen." News of the crownings of the "King" and "Queen" of Hollywood received world-wide coverage.

Gable did not allow his new title to distort his perceptions of himself. "I eat and sleep and go to the bathroom like everybody else," he said. "There's no special light that shines inside me and makes me a star. I'm just a lucky slob from Ohio." He continued his habit of never being late on the movie set; in fact, he was usually five or 10 minutes early. Always nice to his co-workers, he made an effort to help newcomers overcome nervousness. When asked about his acting, he'd respond: "I stand in front of a camera and talk and make faces."

While most movie stars of Gable's stature were known to spend their

(Left) Carole Lombard learned how to shoot a 20-gauge Winchester rifle so she could go hunting with Gable. (Below) Gable owned a station wagon which he used on hunting and fishing trips. In this 1937 photograph, Gable types a letter in the rear of the vehicle.

time between scenes in the privacy of their dressing rooms, Gable visited with his stand-ins, wardrobe men, electricians, sound men and other workers on the set. His dressing room door was always open to visitors. He enjoyed ribbing people, but only those he liked, and it was always out of friendliness. Whenever he overheard a statement of exaggeration, he would quip: "Yeah, that's what the girl said to the sailor!"

Gable seldom found himself the victim of jealousy during his rise to stardom. He was always considerate of his peers and had a calming effect on nervous young actresses. When a reporter asked Spencer Tracy why he considered Gable "the greatest guy in the business," his reply was that "he's a *man* before he's an actor; talks like a man, thinks like a man and never talks movies."

Gable did not display any bad feelings about the rise to stardom of Robert Taylor, an actor on his own lot. Instead, Gable helped Taylor gain membership into a small, but exclusive, duck hunting club in northern California.

For her part, Carole Lombard made sure that Gable didn't let the success of *Test Pilot* or his recent crowning as "King" inflate his ego. Rather than call him "King," she called him by his nicknames—"Pa," "Pappy" and "Moose." She continually reminded him of the fiasco *Parnell* had been. She went so far as to distribute leaflets at MGM (which she had printed) that read: "If you think Gable is the world's greatest actor, see him in *Parnell*. You'll never forget it. If Parnell was as woozy a goof

Spencer Tracy and Myrna Loy co-starred with Gable in Test Pilot *in 1938, the year Gable was named "King" of Hollywood and she was selected "Queen."*

as Gable portrayed him in that picture, Ireland still wouldn't be free."

Carole, herself, never developed a "star complex." She regarded herself as having been extremely fortunate to have reached stardom. Other girls, she said, given the same opportunities, could have achieved the same status. She had few complaints.

Studio photographers took advantage of Lombard's attitude. She allowed them to take publicity pictures whenever they wished. While many female stars avoided candid camera shots, fearful of showing an un-retouched wrinkle, Carole always posed graciously. She enjoyed seeing herself in "crazy" poses. "It's O.K. by me," she would say.

Carole studied the photographs taken of her with no make-up. How could she improve her looks? She decided to capitalize on her sunken cheeks, high forehead and thin hair. She tried to be as natural as possible. She used plain soap and water on her skin and didn't bother with fancy hairdos. The "Carole Lombard look"—hollow cheeks, winging eyebrows, wavy hair with high forehead—became the new vogue.

Carole was a distinctive beauty with great personal charm. Her wit and humor earned her the title of "Screwball Girl No. 1 of the Screen." Not only did she become America's most talented and sophisticated comedienne, she was also rated as one of Hollywood's best-dressed women and was noted for being perfectly groomed. Much of her personal wardrobe was designed especially for her.

By 1937, Carole was the highest paid female star in Hollywood, and reported an income of $465,000—impressive even by today's standards, and absolutely fantastic for the thirties. Of these earnings, she was able to keep only $50,000: approximately $339,000 had gone for federal and state taxes, and the rest for agent fees and business expenses. Russell Birdwell, chief publicist for David O. Selznick Studios, to which Carole was under contract, took advantage of her huge tax payments by publicizing that fact and quoting her as being *happy* to pay them. This gave her plenty of national publicity and brought her a note of thanks from President Roosevelt.

Birdwell also arranged for another Lombard publicity stunt—and she fully cooperated. To publicize her film with James Stewart, *Made for Each Other,* and other Selznick pictures, she worked as a press agent for one week at Selznick International New Bureau. Carole installed a fire bell to summon secretaries and had a siren at her side to announce her presence to Selznick 400 yards away. She explained: "A star spends a lot of time sitting in on story conferences, and others, but never on exploitation and publicity. These departments are important—as important as any of the others. No star should neglect them."

Gable spent the Christmas of 1938 with Carole, her mother, Bessie, and her brothers at a family party at her home. His presents to her were a huge plaster statue of himself and a beautiful yellow Cadillac convertible.

(Above) Gable chats with director Jack Conway on a movie set in 1938. (Below) Carole Lombard's love for Gable couldn't keep her away from the set of his film, Too Hot to Handle, *even on this cold night in 1938.*

Carole Lombard's striking beauty is reflected in this portrait photo. "The Carole Lombard Look" is still being copied by women today.

Carole, still under contract to Selznick, was one of many stars who hoped to win the role of Scarlett O'Hara in *Gone With the Wind,* a movie based on Margaret Mitchell's best-selling novel about the Civil War. Selznick bought the screen rights for $50,000—at that time a record-breaking price. The book about the Old South, its masters and slaves, gentlemen and ladies fair, sectionalism, and a civilization "gone with the wind" had great style, fine characterization, frankness, beauty and a romantic plot. Selznick, the youthful son-in-law of MGM's Louis B. Mayer, was very particular in his casting of the film. It was to be a block-buster—the biggest picture of all time.

There was considerable publicity and speculation as to who would be awarded the coveted role of Scarlett. Joan Crawford, Bette Davis, Katherine Hepburn, Lana Turner, Paulette Goddard, Loretta Young, Jean Arthur, Miriam Hopkins, Tallulah Bankhead, Claudette Colbert, Ann Sheridan, Susan Hayward, Joan Bennett and Irene Dunne—all were mentioned as candidates. Some were granted screentests.

Massive attention was also focused on the role of Rhett Butler. Mail from the public strongly favored Clark Gable. Ronald Colman, Errol Flynn and Gary Cooper were also under consideration. Cooper almost got the part, but he had just signed a contract with Goldwyn Studios. Goldwyn refused to "loan" him out to MGM. Gable was chosen instead.

Clark was, at first, reluctant to play Rhett Butler. He knew that the public, after reading the best-selling novel, had a preconceived idea of the kind of Rhett Butler they wanted to see on the screen. "Suppose I came up empty? Suppose I didn't produce?" Gable pondered.

Many letter-writers urged Gable to accept the role. "He [Rhett] was so obviously written for Gable," they claimed. The myth that author Mitchell had Gable in mind when writing *Gone With the Wind* was widespread. "This is not true," explained Gable. "She got her idea for the book and was writing it while I was a laborer in Oklahoma oil fields." In fact, Gable recalled that upon first reading the book his reaction was enthusiastic and immediate. He said: "What a part for Ronald Colman!"

Gable actually had little choice as to whether he would or would not play Rhett Butler. His MGM contract did not allow him to select his own roles. The company, in full control of his film career, "loaned" him out to Selznick to play Rhett Butler. MGM put up $1,250,000 for a 50% share of

It was an historic moment for Hollywood on August 25, 1938, when Gable, David O. Selznick (standing) and Louis B. Mayer signed the contract for Gone With the Wind.

the profits. However, MGM itself had no control whatsoever over the actual making of the film. Selznick International, smaller than MGM, secured bank loans and produced it at its own studio without any MGM workers. The picture cost $4,250,000.

The MGM-Selznick agreement had been finalized early in 1938, but official announcement was delayed until August of that year. Gable, who had finished *Too Hot to Handle,* in which his co-star was Myrna Loy, was working on *Idiot's Delight* with Norma Shearer during the negotiations with Selznick.

When told that he had been selected to play the male lead in Margaret Mitchell's epic, Gable began rigorous preparation. "I started out with the idea of knowing Rhett as well as I know myself. I lived with him day after day, reading and rereading *Gone With the Wind,* underlining each sentence that revealed a facet of his many-sided character." He put in months of "unrelenting preparation."

Rhett Butler—a gambler, murderer and cynic—was strong-willed, a polished gentleman, and his own worst enemy. He was a mellow blend of good and bad, and had a charming sense of humor.

Vivien Leigh was chosen to play Scarlett O'Hara in Gone With the Wind *after Selznick conducted a two-year talent search.*

The 1037-page novel was translated into a film that ran three hours and 45 minutes, the longest motion picture made to that date. Laboring over the script were Sidney Howard, F. Scott Fitzgerald, Ben Hecht, Selznick, and several others. Much rewriting was done. When the film went into production, many problems arose and, by the time the movie had finished shooting, five directors had contributed their services.

The actors presented problems themselves. Gable refused to speak with a southern accent. He was also concerned about the selection and fit of the clothes he would wear in the film. Until now, Gable had supervised his own costumes for all of his films. He was used to working with one particular tailor, but the man had not been assigned to *Gone With the Wind*. Gable was upset. When Selznick learned of the oversight, he had the tailor hired.

In Gone With the Wind, *Gable played a gambler, cynic and murderer who is attracted to Scarlett O'Hara (Vivien Leigh), daughter of a prosperous plantation owner.*

Reports were heard that Gable was dissatisfied with the selection of a relatively unknown British actress, Vivien Leigh, to play Scarlett. Leigh had been picked after a two-year search. Her superb screentests revealed striking beauty and considerable acting ability. Though temperamental on the set, her acting soon shone through. If Gable was dissatisfied, he apparently changed his opinion when the film was finished. In an article he wrote in *Woman's Home Companion,* in 1940, he said: "I had no difficulty visualizing Miss Leigh as Scarlett. My thanks are here publicly expressed to Miss Leigh for making it a pleasure to believe the part of Rhett."

During the 122 days she was on the set of *Gone With the Wind,* Vivien Leigh made no secret of her feelings about certain scenes. If she found a situation implausible or the dialogue silly, she openly stated her opinions. At one point, Vivien was upset about the dismissal of director George Cukor. MGM and Gable had reportedly been unhappy with Cukor. He was running behind schedule, placing too much camera emphasis on Vivien Leigh and not enough on Gable, forsaking a grand spectacle by shooting too many intimate details, and complaining about Gable's southern accent. Given the opportunity to choose a replacement for Cukor, Gable chose Victor Fleming. Although Fleming became a target for Miss Leigh's temper, he managed to handle her quite well.

Needless to say, *Gone With the Wind* considerably enhanced the Gable image. He became a greater star than ever before and, as such, became the subject of numerous newspaper and magazine articles. During the filming, *Photoplay* magazine ran a controversial article about unwed couples living together. The article mentioned Gable and Lombard, Robert Taylor and Barbara Stanwyck, Charlie Chaplin and Paulette Goddard, Constance Bennett and Gilbert Roland. Living together out of wedlock was not a popular practice in the 1930s and considerable pressure was put on the studios to "get these lovers married." Louis B. Mayer felt that it would be in MGM's interest for Gable and Lombard to become man and wife. So Mayer granted Gable a substantial salary increase and advanced him money to pay off Ria, who was holding out for at least $300,000 in her settlement demands. The financial agreement was finally concluded: Ria was to receive $286,000 after taxes. She went to Reno to obtain the divorce. It was granted on March 8, 1939.

In all, Gable's divorce from Ria, including the three-year separation payments, cost him more than half-a-million dollars. Ironically enough, when Gable had first signed a big contract at MGM, Hedda Hopper told him he'd "probably go right out and spend it on some woman." He retorted: "No woman is ever going to get a penny out of me. I'm going to salt it away. I figure I have just two years at this sum, and baby, I'm going to save every penny."

Divorced from Ria Langham and legally free to marry, Gable had only to find the *time* to marry the woman he loved: Carole Lombard. Through Howard Strickling, MGM's publicity boss, he arranged for Otto Winkler,

Gable, as Rhett Butler, poses for a publicity shot for Gone With the Wind, *which many consider his best picture.*

In the splendor of 70mm. wide screen and full stereophonic sound!

DAVID O. SELZNICK'S PRODUCTION OF MARGARET MITCHELL'S

"GONE WITH THE WIND"

Winner of Ten Academy Awards

STARRING

CLARK GABLE
VIVIEN LEIGH
LESLIE HOWARD
OLIVIA de HAVILLAND

RE-RELEASED BY
METRO-GOLDWYN-MAYER INC.
MGM

DIRECTED BY
VICTOR FLEMING · SIDNEY HOWARD

SCREEN
PLAY BY

A SELZNICK INTERNATIONAL PICTURE · VICTOR FLEMING

MUSIC BY
MAX STEINER · IN 70 mm. WIDE SCREEN STEREOPHONIC SOUND METROCOLOR

This famous poster advertising Gone With the Wind is much sought by collectors of movie memorabilia.

an MGM publicist, to make wedding plans. Both Clark and Carole wanted a quiet, simple wedding, completely free of fanfare and publicity.

Although *Gone With the Wind* was shot over a period of seven and one-half months in 1939, there had been periods of time when Gable's presence was not required. When he learned that he would have two days off on March 29 and 30, he and Carole set the date for their marriage— March 29, 1939.

When the day of the wedding arrived, Clark left his rented home in North Hollywood at 4:00 a.m. He picked up Carole and Winkler and the trio departed for Kingman, Arizona, where they immediately went to the town hall to obtain a marriage license. Carole gave her age as 29 (she was really 30), and Clark as 38. From the town hall they went to the home of the minister of the First Methodist-Episcopal Church, where the ceremony was to be performed. Clark and Carole, who had been wearing

Clark, 38, and Carole, 30, on their wedding day in 1939. They eloped to Kingman, Arizona.

casual clothes, changed into dress attire. He donned a blue serge suit, white shirt and printed tie, she a light-grey flannel suit, tapered at the waist, with a grey and white polka-dot vest.

Carole telephoned her mother immediately after the ceremony to

Carole Lombard and Clark Gable pose with their wedding cake in the MGM commissary following their marriage in March, 1939.

reveal the news. Clark, taking the phone from her, interjected: "This is your new son-in-law, Mom." With arms around each other, the bride and bridegroom left the church and sped away. Winkler was behind the wheel.

After traveling several miles, Gable had Winkler stop the car. He got out and telephoned the news of the marriage to the MGM publicity department. Telegrams immediately were sent to columnist Louella Parsons, and her publisher, William Randolph Hearst.

Later during the trip, Clark and Carole stopped at a highway Harvey House restaurant. They ate thick steaks for their wedding dinner and then continued the drive back to Los Angeles. They arrived at Carole's home in Bel-Air at about 3:00 a.m., almost 24 hours after they had left. They napped for a few hours, and refreshed themselves for the obligatory press conference.

Reporters began arriving early. MGM police stood guard outside the house so that only the press could gain admission. The Gables explained that they would be unable to take a honeymoon because of their picture-making commitments. When asked if they planned to have children, Carole smiled, giggling, and Gable appeared embarrassed. Carole said she could cook, "Damn well, too." Asked if they thought their film careers and marriage could mix, Gable replied: "We'd rather not answer that."

And so, the marriage of Clark Gable and Carole Lombard had begun —three years and two months after that memorable evening of January 28, 1936 at the Mayfair Ball.

5
Home on the Ranch

WHEN FIRST MARRIED, Mr. and Mrs. Clark Gable shared their Bel-Air home with Carole's mother and two brothers. Prior to their marriage, the Gables had seen a house in Encino, a suburban Los Angeles area of the San Fernando Valley, with which they both fell in love. The 13-year-old house, set on a 20-acre ranch, was owned by director Raoul Walsh. It was a good buy, but considerable work would have to be done before it could be made livable. The two-story brick and frame house, resembling a Connecticut farmhouse with its tall, brick chimneys, needed new furnishings, a roomier kitchen and the addition of servants' quarters.

Carole anted up the $50,000 cash required to buy the house and acreage, since Gable was faced with $286,000 in payments that he would have to make as part of his divorce settlement. The Gables were delighted with the purchase, especially Clark. "It will be the first home that I've had since I was a boy that I can really call my own," he told Carole. "I think we're going to be very happy here."

The 20-acre ranch included a small stable, a barn, chicken coops and brooders. All buildings on the ranch were painted white with dark green shutters, in New England style.

While still living in Bel-Air, Carole and Clark used all their free time to spruce up the place and supervise the hired workers. Fences were mended, irrigation lines repaired, trees pruned. Carole shopped for furniture, antiques, and other decorative pieces.

Early in July of 1939, when the refurbishing was complete, the Gables moved into their new home. It was not a spectacular showcase when compared to the palatial estates of many Hollywood film stars. It had no swimming pool, no tennis court, no film projection room. But, the home had ample space and much charm. Gable had a gun room on the main floor which housed a gun collection consisting of a few dozen antique pistols and rifles. The huge living room was decorated simply. It featured white paneling, canary yellow carpeting, windows draped with gay English prints, and two large yellow sofas flanked by wing-back chairs. The bricks on the fireplace were white. A colonial style staircase led to the second floor.

The dining room, finished in natural pine and resembling a typical Early American tavern, had greyish-white beams and a brick fireplace. A chandelier of oil lamps was wired for electricity. The new couple was not satisfied with the "antiquing" job that had been done on the long, tavern-type table which dominated the room, and so the Gables gave it an aged look by studding out their cigarettes on it and beating it with a heavy chain. Captain chairs were placed around the table. Near an open bar counter stood a game table. Pink china and rare prints of horses lined the walls.

This postcard of the ranch home of Gable and Lombard is a collector's item to-day. The home, set on 20 acres of land, was bought in 1939 for $50,000.

Upstairs, Clark and Carole both had their own master bedroom suite. Gable's room was masculine: brown and beige predominated. A large green couch, an old pine desk given to him by David O. Selznick after the filming of *Gone With the Wind,* and a dictionary stand with an unabridged dictionary filled the room. Bookcases lined the walls. Gable's dressing room, large enough to contain his extensive wardrobe, was mirrored. Beige marble, with glass shelves holding antique bottles, highlighted the bathroom.

Carole's bedroom suite was very feminine. The deep rug, the goatskin throw rugs, the sofa and chairs—all were white, Carole's favorite color.

Carole and Clark relax on the steps of their Encino ranch home. The home resembled a Connecticut farmhouse.

Her mahogany fourposter bed, with a canopy of starched white cloth, had matching mahogany bedside tables. The dressing room was lined with mirrors. Closet doors were lined with cedar. The large mirrored bathroom was also almost exclusively white.

Situated in a highly wooded, somewhat secluded and hilly area of the valley, the Gable home was not visible from the road. They were now afforded the privacy for which they had yearned. But the Gable home was not completely isolated—not by any means. It was only 12 miles from the heart of Hollywood, and a mere 45-minute drive from their film studios.

Clark and Carole enjoyed spending quiet evenings in the comfort of their home. They delighted in horseback riding and loved relaxing on the wide back porch, furnished with yellow tables and chairs, or in Clark's comfortable gun room. Clark spent a great deal of time near the garage tinkering with his cars. High-powered motors fascinated him and he was a talented mechanic. He changed cars every year or so.

Carole filled the house with gaiety and laughter. She centered activity and conversation around Clark's likes and dislikes. When he was silent or moody, she would clown around until he smiled again. Gable adored her. To him, she was "the most exciting, amusing, desirable woman in the world."

By Hollywood standards, the Gables did little entertaining except for an occasional small dinner party and their annual, more formal dinner for several studio executives and other important film folk. In addition, each summer, they threw a party for about 20 of their closest friends. Gable had always disliked night clubs, big parties and formal dinners, and equally hated having to dress for them. He much preferred inviting a few close friends to the ranch for dinner or drinks.

The Gables' most frequent ranch guests included Phil Berg (Clark's agent), Eddie Mannix of MGM, Mr. and Mrs. Al Menasco (an auto dealer), Mr. and Mrs. Howard Strickling, Mr. and Mrs. Andy Devine, Mr. and Mrs. Howard Hawks, Mr. and Mrs. Norris Goff (Abner of the Lum and Abner comedy team), Mr. and Mrs. Buster Collier, Mr. and Mrs. Harry Fleishmann and Mr. and Mrs. Walter Lang. On one occasion, Gable gave the Oscar he had won for *It Happened One Night* to Lang's son, Richard, age 12, after the boy expressed his admiration of it.

Clark and Carole were living a full life. They were very much in love. Although his divorce from Ria had cost him a considerable sum, Gable was now recovering and becoming a very wealthy man. Clark and Carole's combined income was at least $550,000 a year, not including the return on their investments, but they lived conservatively. Living expenses on the ranch reached only $16,000 a year for servants, food, repairs, taxes, and miscellaneous items. The ranch did not really pay for itself, but it wasn't expected to. It was a way of life for Clark and Carole. The ranch, with its chickens, turkeys, cows, and mixed assortment of fruit trees, brought much joy to Gable. He often rose early, hitched the mule to a road scraper, worked with the tractor, or tended to his vegetables. Carole pitched in and occasionally took care of the chickens and the flower garden.

One day, while Gable was working in the barn, a cow charged him and knocked him a good distance. He was shaken but not hurt. Later that day, Carole, who had witnessed the incident, bought a red toreador's outfit which she impishly presented to Clark at dinner that night. Not long afterward, Gable pulled one of his own gags on her. When she proudly displayed a new riding outfit, showing off the breeches and shiny boots, he promised her a fine new thoroughbred saddle horse. The horse was delivered the next morning. Excitedly, she rushed to the barn—only to find an old swaybacked horse that might be found in a comedy movie.

Although he could afford hired help, Gable preferred to do much of the manual labor himself. One August morning in 1939, Gable was quietly relaxing at home. Carole had already gone to the studio to pose for publicity pictures and Clark went into the orchard to dig irrigation ditches for trees he was nursing. A ring on his finger felt too tight. He returned to the house to remove the ring and get a pack of cigarettes. As he pulled the ring from his finger, he glanced at the mirror on his dressing room wall. He noticed a door opening slowly behind him. A foot appeared and then a hat brim. A rough-looking man, one hand in his pocket, slipped into the room. He had not yet seen Gable, who quickly clouted him behind the ear. The strong blow knocked the young man down. Gable, frisking the youth, found one of his own guns. He dragged the young man, who appeared to be approximately 21 years old, down the stairs and into the kitchen.

"What are you doing here?" Gable demanded.

"I wanted some money," the young man replied.

"You have a peculiar way of asking for it!" Gable snapped. "There are better ways."

Gable demanded an apology.

"I'm not sorry," was the thief's response as he made a lunge for the door. Gable tackled him and held him prisoner until the police arrived.

Later, Clark discovered that the youth had been on the ranch the previous night, peeked through a window, and saw the gun collection. The boy bedded down in Gable's car, thus sharing the garage with Gable's boxer watchdog. In the morning, the would-be robber came to the kitchen door and identified himself to Gable's housekeeper-cook as one of Clark's friends. As the housekeeper-cook searched for Gable, the youth sneaked into the gun room and snatched one of the guns.

Gable had called his watchdog "Tuffy" and "Old Dependable." After the attempted robbery, Carole suggested a new name: "Old Sweetie."

The pleasant life on the ranch that first summer was soon interrupted again—this time by Carole's appendectomy at the Cedars of Lebanon Hospital. Gable took a room next to hers and stayed there throughout her hospitalization. When Carole was released from the hospital and regained her strength, she resumed her schedule.

Carole, who had been very busy working in pictures, did not have much time for domestic chores. And so, in addition to the housekeeper-cook, the Gables hired a butler-handyman to serve drinks and occasionally drive for them. Jean Garceau, who had up to now been Carole's personal secretary, now worked for Clark as well. Home life for the Gables continued smoothly. Some of their happiest times were spent over dinner. Gable loved thick steaks, baked potatoes filled with butter, baked beans and spareribs. Stewed chicken and dumplings, corn bread, homemade ice cream, chocolate cake, and hamburgers with onions were also favorites. At dinner, Carole insisted on formal service even when dining alone with her husband. The table was set with exquisite Waterford crystal and Spode. They used exquisite antique silver flatware, the blades of which were polished daily.

The personalities of Clark and Carole contrasted enough to make them a very interesting and compatible couple. Gable was a good-natured, easy-going, quiet—although sometimes moody—and calm type of person. Carole was chattier, somewhat high-strung and nervous. They continually played jokes on each other and delighted in one another's company. They refused to discuss their work at home, except in their secretary's office. The one exception was Gable's reluctance to attend the world premiere of *Gone With the Wind* on December 15, 1939, in Atlanta, Georgia, the home of author Margaret Mitchell.

Plans for a massive three-day affair had been made. The governor of Georgia had gone so far as to declare the occasion a state holiday. Gable, always self-conscious and shy in crowds, dreaded the scheduled parade and other social activities. Moreover, he wasn't too happy with David O. Selznick's handling of problems in filming the picture. And Selznick had a hand in the extravagant affair being planned by MGM.

Carole encouraged Clark to attend the opening. He reluctantly agreed to go—but only if she would accompany him. MGM wasn't pleased with this idea. Carole had been in no way involved in the making of *Gone With the Wind*. She, herself, feared that her presence might divert some of the attention from her husband. But, when Gable learned that Vivien Leigh would be escorted by her lover, Laurence Olivier, he demanded that MGM allow Carole to accompany him. The studio chartered a DC-3 passenger plane, and the Gables, along with publicist Otto Winkler, flew to Atlanta.

Thousands lined Atlanta streets to welcome the star couple. Some wore Civil War costumes; strolling musicians played "Dixie." Gable and Lombard sat perched in the back of an open Packard convertible and waved to the spectators as the motorcade drove the seven miles from the airport to the hotel.

That evening, a gala dress ball was held, for which 8,000 tickets (at $10 each) were sold by southern society belles, the proceeds going to charity. Vivien Leigh and Olivia de Havilland appeared dressed in the costumes they had worn in *Gone With the Wind*. Gable and Lombard sat quietly in a box. Carole, looking lovely in a black velvet evening dress, was approached by many autograph hunters.

Atlanta's Loew's Grand Theater served as the choice for the premiere showing of *Gone With the Wind*. The demand for tickets was great. Nearly 40,000 tickets were requested, but Loew's Grand had a seating capacity of only 2,000. All had been sold at $10 each.

The premiere was a typical gala Hollywood bash of the thirties. The front of the theater was decorated to look like Twelve Oaks, one of the

Carole and Clark attend the premiere of Gone With the Wind *in Atlanta in December, 1939, part of a three-day celebration in author Margaret Mitchell's hometown. (Inset) Gable arrives in Atlanta for the premiere of* Gone With the Wind. *He was greeted by many thousands.*

mansions in the movie. Many big stars attended; scores of newsmen, photographers, movie cameramen and radio news reporters were scattered about.

When the Gables arrived—Gable dressed in white tie and tails, Carole in a champagne satin gown—the fans went wild. Police had to restrain them.

"This is Margaret Mitchell's night and *your* night," Gable said, as he addressed the crowd. "Just let me be a spectator, going in to see *Gone With the Wind.*" The Gables sat next to Margaret Mitchell and her husband, John Marsh, during the showing.

Gable said he didn't realize how well he had done in the picture until the Atlanta premiere. Audience reaction was his gauge. Margaret Mitchell said he played Rhett Butler just as she had envisioned the part.

The premiere was a fantastic success and the movie was acclaimed by the critics. *The New York Herald Tribune* reported, "It is a monumental picture! . . . Standing alone in its class." *Time* said it was "the best of Gable's career without a doubt." *Variety* commented: "Gable gives the performance of the year. And Vivien Leigh is not far behind." *Photoplay's* observation was that "Clark Gable has only to be himself, so perfectly cast he is as Rhett Butler."

"Rhett Butler always will remain among the most memorable roles I have played on the screen, although I sincerely believe that Fletcher Christian in *Mutiny on the Bounty* was a part of equal calibre," Gable said later. "It was the unprecedented public interest in Rhett that made it a difficult and frightening role to tackle. *Gone With the Wind* belongs to the public, not Hollywood."

After three days of frenzied celebration, the Gables returned to Los Angeles. A story, now legendary, circulated. It told of a woman who approached the reservations desk at the Atlanta hotel in which the Gables had stayed and asked if she could rent the room the stars had just vacated.

The clerk said: "Yes. After the room is cleaned and the bed is made up."

"I'll take it just as it is," she said, "and please make sure they don't change the sheets. I want it exactly as it is." This was but one instance of many that indicates the adoration in which Clark Gable and Carole Lombard were held.

After the Atlanta premiere, there was much talk about the picture and the celebration that accompanied it. Clark would talk only about Carole. "You should have seen the way they looked at Carole. You never saw anybody so beautiful," he repeated again and again.

Back in Los Angeles, the Gables were now asked to attend the Hollywood premiere of *Gone With the Wind.* Again, Gable was reluctant to attend. Carole joked that if he refused, she would go with his stand-in, Lew Smith. Carole succeeded in persuading him, but Gable shunned the post-premiere party that Selznick hosted at the Trocadero. He and his wife went directly home after the screening.

Carole, who had appeared in *Nothing Sacred* and *Made for Each Other* for Selznick, was under contract to do another film with Selznick. She received a letter from Selznick asking if she really wanted to make another picture for him. After all, the producer reasoned, Gable was displeased with the treatment Selznick had given him during *Gone With the Wind*. "All through the picture he [Gable] was frank in expressing his suspicions that I intended to do him in, and I kept pleading with him to wait until the picture was finished and then tell me his opinion," Selznick wrote Carole. "I was under the impression that he was delighted with the final result, but he apparently disassociates me from this final result, if I am to judge from what has been reported back to me, and from items in the press."

Gable usually took long vacations between pictures. He spent much of that time hunting small game.

Selznick added, "I certainly recognize the awkward position you are in, and cannot expect to come out on the right side when your loyalties are divided. . . . The decision is entirely yours. You would suffer much more from repercussions in your personal life than would I; and I can stand it if you can."

Carole declined the offer to make another movie for Selznick. Instead, she continued her four-picture contract with RKO at $150,000 per film.

With *Gone With the Wind* premieres out of the way, the Gables concentrated on their first Christmas together. They held a small dinner party. Guests included Clark's father and stepmother and Carole's mother and two brothers.

Seated near a tall evergreen tree sprayed white, Clark and Carole tenderly exchanged gifts. His gift to her was a ruby heart to wear around her neck. She gave him sexy, white silk pajamas and a matching robe. On New Year's day, 1940, Carole made a firm resolution: to get pregnant. She

Gable usually dressed casually when he was on the ranch. He preferred staying at home to the Hollywood night life.

even stopped horseback riding, suspecting that it might prevent her from conceiving.

She continued to fish and hunt with Clark, however. They took frequent trips to Oregon with the Fleischmanns, and stayed at the Gibson family's We-Ask-U Inn sportsman's lodge on the Rogue River.

In late January, 1940, the Gables went on a duck hunting trip to the La Grulla Gun Club in Baja, California, near the mountains below Ensenada. Having little luck there, they headed further south to a more primitive area to try for geese. After a couple of luckless days, they decided to head back for La Grulla. On the way, they encountered a heavy rainstorm, and their custom-made Dodge station wagon skidded off the road and got stuck in the mud. They spent the night in the back of the Dodge bundled up in their sleeping bags. All they had to eat was a birthday cake presented to Clark on his 39th birthday by the lodge owners in whose quarters they had stayed the night before. They devoured it.

Otto Winkler, who was to join the Gables briefly to supervise the taking of publicity pictures, became concerned when he did not hear from the couple and was unable to locate them. A chartered plane took him to Ensenada. Not finding the Gables there, he wired MGM for help. The news broke through wire services that Gable and Lombard were missing in Mexico.

When the rain stopped the next morning, two men in a truck happened to pass the Gables' disabled station wagon. They towed it out of the mud. When the star couple returned to the La Grulla Gun Club, they learned that Winkler had persuaded the Mexican government to organize a search party. When Mexican officials were told of the Gables' "rescue," they became irritated. This was, they believed, a cheap publicity stunt. MGM was annoyed as well, and they fired Winkler, but Gable saw to it that he was quickly reinstated.

Back in Los Angeles, Gable learned that he had been nominated for an Academy Award for his performance in *Gone With the Wind*. Although he was widely praised for his convincing portrayal of Rhett Butler, he did not win the Oscar. It went to Robert Donat for his role in *Goodbye, Mr. Chips*. Vivien Leigh won the Oscar for Best Actress, one of the 10 Academy Awards *Gone With the Wind* received. The others included: Best Picture, Best Director (Victor Fleming), Best Screenplay (Sidney Howard) and Best Supporting Actress (Hattie McDaniel).

Many movie industry insiders realized that Gable's loss of the Academy Award was a result of MGM's casting a bloc of its votes for Donat. *Goodbye, Mr. Chips* needed help at the box office; *Gone With the Wind* did not.

Hailed as the greatest picture of all time, *Gone With the Wind* enjoyed a long run with the record crowds. MGM acquired all rights to the film and continued to reissue it every few years. By 1975, the picture had grossed $70 million in the United States and Canada, and more than $135,000,000 world-wide. Gable, who had been paid his standard salary of $4,500 per week, could have become a *very* wealthy man had he had a percentage arrangement in his contract.

Following the success of *Gone With the Wind*, Gable's salary jumped to $7,500 per week for 40 weeks. Effective January 25, 1940, he would be earning $300,000 per year. With Lombard making that much, and possibly more because of the percentage clause in her contract, the Gables were very financially secure. They could have afforded a Beverly Hills mansion, but continued to find joy at the Encino ranch.

Money no longer a consideration, Gable treated himself to a lavish wardrobe. His garage was now occupied by two expensive cars in addition to his Dodge station wagon.

During his spare time, Gable kept busy caring for his chickens, citrus trees, dairy cows and doves. The doves were the very ones Carole had given him after the Mayfair Ball in 1936, and were housed in a special pen.

At the studio, Gable had just finished *Strange Cargo* with Joan Crawford. He played a tough convict and she a brothel gal. He was now working on *Boom Town* with Spencer Tracy. This picture, released on August 30, 1940, ignited memories in Gable of the rough, crude world of oil drilling. Claudette Colbert and Hedy Lamarr were his co-stars. *The New York Times'* review said that Gable "looks and acts like an oil man—brassy, direct and tough."

Gossipers hinted that Gable would surely become involved with the sexy Hedy Lamarr, who was well known for her nude swim scene in *Ecstasy.* But not so. He was too much in love with Carole.

At the time, Lombard was busy making *They Knew What They Wanted* for RKO. It co-starred Charles Laughton and William Gargan. This was Carole's third successive dramatic role, preceded by *In Name Only* with Cary Grant and *Vigil in the Night* with Brian Aherne. Some scenes were filmed in the Napa Valley vineyards near San Francisco, and wanting to be together as much as possible, Gable went with her whenever his schedule allowed. They found time for hunting and fishing when Carole wasn't needed on the set.

Gable soon returned to MGM for another film with Hedy Lamarr, *Comrade X.* He played a cynical newspaper reporter who falls in love with a Russian streetcar motorwoman.

Carole, meanwhile, went to work in *Mr. and Mrs. Smith,* an RKO comedy in which she appeared with Robert Montgomery, Gene Raymond and Jack Carson.

The Gables spent much free time duck hunting at Fleischmann's Lodge and Gun Club in Bakersfield. Other guests at the lodge included Robert Taylor and Robert Stack, friends of the Gables. For the most part, the lodge was a pleasant and effective retreat from Hollywood for Clark and Carole.

Carole learned to accustom herself to outdoor life. Once, on a weekend outing in Arizona with their friends, the Al Menascos, she stepped on a rattlesnake. She leaped to the side just in time. Al and Clark fired several shots, killing the snake. On another occasion, while duck hunting at Laguna Hanson, a lake high in the mountains, Carole was stung by a bee, and later was plagued by a bad case of poison ivy rash. She was confined to bed for several days.

(Above) In 1940, Gable appeared with Joan Crawford in Strange Cargo. They remained close friends in real life for several years. (Below) Hedy Lamarr first appeared with Gable in Boom Town in 1940. Later that year they co-starred in Comrade X.

Carole and Clark are shown here with their horse, Melody. Carole gave up horseback riding in the hopes of conceiving a child.

When she was well enough to travel, the Gables prepared for their trip home. Paul Mantz, a stunt pilot and technical advisor for films, including Gable's *Test Pilot,* had flown them to the lake in his Sikorsky S-38 Twin Engine Amphibian. As they were about to begin the return trip, there was a scare. The plane had been loaded with two cases of ammunition and heavy battery. As Mantz readied for the take-off, he noticed the dense forest surrounding the water. He knew that the plane would not clear the treetops. Mantz stopped the aircraft, unloaded the heavy cargo, and took off—this time the craft barely cleared the trees. Carole turned to Clark and said, "Please, let's never travel in separate planes. Whenever I fly, I want you with me."

In December, 1940, the Gables traveled by rail to Johns Hopkins Medical Center in Baltimore. Carole underwent a gynecological examination; she had been troubled about her inability to conceive. The doctors found nothing wrong. While there, Gable had the physicians examine his shoulder. It had pained him intermittently ever since a wall of wooden bricks caved in on him during the filming of an earthquake scene in *San Francisco*. Doctors discovered that an infected tooth was further aggravating his shoulder. They promptly removed the tooth, gave him massage treatments and put him on an exercise program to strengthen the muscles surrounding the shoulder.

Following the Johns Hopkins tests, the Gables travelled a bit south to Washington, D.C. MGM had arranged a grand tour of the capital, including a visit with President and Mrs. Franklin D. Roosevelt. At the White House, the Gables sat in on one of the President's famous fireside chat radio broadcasts. FDR warned of the threat of Germany and the importance of supporting England and Russia against the Nazis.

Later, President and Mrs. Roosevelt talked with the Gables for about 30 minutes. He complimented Carole on her support of the income-tax system and for publicizing that fact. A movie fan, the President then questioned Clark about *Gone With the Wind*. He also sought the Gables' opinions on how the film industry could help the country and its current emergency.

Clark and Carole Gable, both very patriotic, were very excited about meeting and chatting with the President. It was the highlight of their trip and an experience they would be proud to talk about for years to come.

6
Tragic Ending

IN MARCH, 1941, CLARK AND CAROLE celebrated their second wedding anniversary. Gable was filming *They Met in Bombay* with Rosalind Russell on the MGM lot. Carole planned a party: she arranged for the Brown Derby to deliver succulent roast turkey with all the trimmings. There was two of everything—refreshments, presents and gags—to symbolize two years of marriage.

Two years of marriage, plus three years together before exchanging marital vows, equalled a five-year relationship for Clark Gable and Carole Lombard. This defied Hollywood's strong belief that film stars could not be compatible mates. Pressures of making films and concentrating on careers, ego clashes and professional jealousy were always cited as inevitable and destructive. But from all appearances, Clark and Carole had the ideal marriage. How could this be?

Friends pointed to Carole's voluntary conversion from a lover of parties to a lover of the outdoors. Clark was most important to her and she did everything possible to please him. She gave him love and companionship, she made him feel like a man, a young man having fun, and she made him laugh. She even took a leave of absence from her film career in the hope of having a baby.

Both had the highest professional standing. Financial problems, notorious for wrecking marriages, were absent. Both were healthy. Both made time for each other. In fact, Carole planned her work schedule so that she would only be working when Clark was working. They wanted the time together.

But the ranch was no longer the refuge it had once been. Maps of movie stars' residences, hawked on Hollywood streets, noted the location

93

of the Gable home. Tour buses stuffed with sightseers often stopped in front of the ranch. Fans sometimes scaled the high fence that bordered the property, hoping to get a glimpse of Clark or Carole. Several times, the MGM studio police had to be summoned to remove trespassers. Eventually, Gable installed a fence with an electrically controlled gate. All visitors had now to identify themselves by using the communications system provided for that purpose.

Clark is shown here with his father, Will Gable, for whom he built a home in 1941. Will moved to California in 1931 after working many years in oil fields.

The Gables began shopping for a new home. They looked at larger, more isolated ranches in areas of California, Arizona, Nevada and Oregon. But they soon abandoned the plan, mostly because they were sentimental about their Encino ranch.

Meanwhile, Gable, encouraged by Carole to become closer to his father, had a house built for his dad in Sherman Oaks, six miles from the ranch. Construction of the modest Cape Cod home began in the spring of 1941, and was completed by July of that year. (Gable had been helping his father all along by sending him $500 a month.)

Gable's 20-acre ranch gave him plenty of room to ride horses through woods and hills. That's Carole striding a fence.

Carole and Clark threw a housewarming party for the senior Gables. Carole was glad to see that Clark was on good terms with his father after so many years of animosity. Although Gable was highly successful in films, his father didn't like the idea of his son being an actor and he maintained that Clark would have been better off working in the oil fields.

Carole's relationship with her family was quite different. She had always been very close with her mother, Bessie, and visited her frequently, along with her two brothers, Stuart and Fred. Gable was fond of his mother-in-law, but he disliked Carole's brothers. He considered them "spongers."

These were mostly happy days for Clark and Carole. They were rarely seen in public. When not off on one of their frequent hunting or fishing trips, they stayed at home for the most part. Both were insatiable readers; Gable particularly loved mystery novels. They sometimes played poker and occasionally hosted a party for a few select friends.

An anecdote often repeated by friends of the Gables described how once, while Clark was reflecting on how fortunate he and his wife had been, he asked her if she could think of anything she really wanted that

Many quiet evenings at home were spent by Carole and Clark during the three years they were together as man and wife. Here, they tend to the fire in the fireplace.

Gable enjoyed watching Carole teach their dog new tricks. They always had several pets on the ranch.

she didn't have. She smiled: "I could use a couple of loads of manure for our fruit trees."

When the Gables did quarrel, it was usually over reports that he was having an affair with some starlet. Carole was not a possessive or jealous woman. She was, in fact, quite understanding. She knew that Gable's rank as America's No. 1 romantic star or sex idol encouraged many women—starlets, extras, stars, and studio secretaries—to make themselves available to him. It was difficult for the 40-year-old Gable to repel these advances from glamorous, adoring young beauties, but Carole remained calm as long as Gable's response was physical rather than emotional.

Numerous reports that Gable slept with scores of starlets, secretaries, chambermaids and waitresses circulated. These were not publicized in newspapers or magazines as were Errol Flynn's escapades with women, but the rumors persisted. Whether or not the stories were true would be known only to those parties who may have been involved. Gable was not the type of man to go around boasting of his affairs. Male sex symbols are always the targets of alleged tales of sexual conquest. A naive observer would probably assume that Gable—because of his status and his opportunities—had his share of extra-marital relations. After all, he was known to appreciate women. But, in any case, his true love was Carole.

The summer and early fall of 1941 found Gable filming *Honky Tonk* with a 21-year-old blonde beauty named Lana Turner. Rumor had it that Lana Turner wanted Clark Gable. The talk sounded so serious that Carole created many occasions to visit Clark on the set. She carefully watched the love scenes between Gable and Turner. She concluded that nothing romantic had developed. The rumors simply provided good publicity for the rising star of Miss Turner.

Honky Tonk, released in the early fall of 1941, won generally favorable reviews for both Gable and Turner. Gable was now anxious to relax, to go hunting with the Fleischmanns. The duck season had opened and the two couples planned to fly to Watertown, South Dakota. When bad weather grounded their plane in Albuquerque, New Mexico, they boarded a train to Kansas City. From Kansas City they flew to Omaha where they changed planes. They arrived in Watertown at 2:00 a.m., immediately changed clothes and drove the 60 miles to the hunting site. It was typical of the hardship they were willing to endure just to go hunting. And as it turned out, the trouble was worth it; they had a wonderful time.

Back in Los Angeles, Carole decided to return to the making of films after a one year's leave. Her inability to conceive had bothered her greatly. Carole's mother, who was active in the Church of Religious Science, had been encouraging Carole to embrace the religion, which she did. But Carole continued to be despondent and, encouraged by her mother and Clark, she decided to resume her film career.

Carole's year-long sabbatical did not diminish her star ranking. She continued to be the cherished subject of numerous newspaper and magazine articles. She was Gable's wife and more—she was still Carole Lombard, and her name and photograph was used in full-page ads to endorse Lux soap, "9 out of 10 screen stars use Lux toilet soap." The ads appeared in leading women's magazines under the heading, "She's Famous—She's Beautiful."

Carole returned to films in grand style. She had top billing with Jack Benny in *To Be or Not to Be*, an anti-Nazi comedy. In the movie, she, portraying a Polish actress, and Benny, playing her actor-husband, struggled against the Nazis in Warsaw of the late 1930s.

Carole, a very patriotic woman, was enthusiastic about making the film. The final days of shooting were close at hand when, on December 7, 1941, the Japanese attacked Pearl Harbor. With America now hurled into the war, Carole was determined to contribute to the country's military effort. She urged Gable to enlist in the Armed Forces; she would join the women's branch of the Army or Navy, or possibly the Red Cross.

Carole asked Clark to write President Roosevelt and offer their services. He did. The President replied: "You are needed where you are," reminding them that entertainment was very greatly needed to maintain the nation's morale.

Carole, however, still insisted that Clark enlist. He was not terribly anxious. He was nearly 41 years of age and, although men up to the age of 44 were draftable, he knew that the younger men were recruited first. As far as MGM was concerned, Gable, earning $7,500 per week, was—along with Mickey Rooney and Spencer Tracy—one of the studio's most valuable assets. Louis B. Mayer and other MGM officials took a dim view of losing Gable, but knew they couldn't keep him out of the service. They hoped he would get a commission rather than being drafted into service. However, Carole didn't want to see Clark get any phony commission through influential sources. Urged on by her, he finally agreed to enlist if MGM approved. MGM contacted Washington War Department officials and the answer they received echoed the President's sentiments: Gable could best serve his country in his present capacity.

Carole finished *To Be or Not to Be* on Christmas Eve. She and Clark hosted a holiday party for servicemen on the MGM lot.

Because of the war, the Gables cut back on gifts to relatives and friends. They notified the people on their Christmas list that they were making donations to the Red Cross and other charities in their names. Clark's Christmas gift to Carole was a pair of diamond and ruby ear clips to match the ruby heart of the previous Christmas. Clark received a slim, solid gold cigarette case from Carole. It was inscribed: "Pa, Dear—I love you—Ma."

Shortly after the Pearl Harbor attack, the movie industry organized

Carole Lombard's fame and beauty were extolled in ads, such as this one in the September, 1941 issue of Good Housekeeping.

the Hollywood Victory Committee to plan entertainment for the U.S. Armed Forces. Gable became chairman of the talent coordinating committee of the Hollywood Victory Canteen. Other members of the committee were Bob Hope, John Garfield, Tyrone Power, Gary Cooper, Ronald Colman, Cary Grant, Jack Benny, Charles Boyer, Myrna Loy, Claudette Colbert, Bette Davis, Ginger Rogers and Irene Dunne.

Early in 1942, Gable was asked to recommend a star to launch Indiana's campaign to sell U.S. Defense Bonds. Carole happened to be a native of Indiana, was between films, and was eager to serve her country. Clark chose her. Carole wanted Gable to accompany her to Indiana, but he was unable to. He had an appointment to go to Washington, D.C. to discuss his particular military situation with General "Hap" Arnold of the Army Air Force. Furthermore, Gable was due to start a film in mid-January, about the same time as the Indiana bond rally.

"Bessie's a Hoosier, too," he said, referring to Carole's mother. "Take her along." Cornwell Jackson, one of Gable's agents, was to accompany Carole and her mother, but when his business commitments made him unavailable, Otto Winkler was persuaded by Gable to take his place.

Carole was reluctant to leave Clark behind: his new picture would again star Lana Turner and rumors once again had begun to circulate.

When Carole, her mother, and Winkler departed from Los Angeles Union Station on January 12, 1942 for the Indiana bond rally, Gable was conspicuously absent. MGM's publicity department stated that he was still in Washington, but insiders claimed that he was in Hollywood and that he and Carole had quarreled over his alleged trysts with Lana Turner and one or two other young females—hence, his absence.

At Union Station, about to board her train, Carole, never known to be overly affectionate or demonstrative with women, hugged her secretary, Jean Garceau, for a long time and kissed her. The blonde actress said, "Take care of my old man for me, will you, Jeanie? You know you'll be working with him more and more now." Carole gave her secretary a series of notes to give to Clark on each day she was to be gone. Mrs. Garceau later said that Carole, who was usually lighthearted and happy, was very depressed that day.

Carole telephoned Gable, who had returned home, when the train arrived in Salt Lake City, Utah. She then made a platform speech urging the purchase of defense bonds. This done, the journey continued. Carole called him from every stop en route to Indiana. She also sent him a wire: "Hey, Pappy, you better get into this man's Army."

The train finally arrived in Indianapolis on the morning of January 15. Carole was rushed, by motorcade, to the State House for a flag-raising ceremony. She again delivered the speech she had been making at train stops along the way. The crowd of nearly 3,000 roared in appreciation as she ended: "Heads up—hands up, America. Let's give a cheer that will be heard in Tokyo and Berlin."

Inside the State House lobby, long lines formed to buy bonds from Lombard. She gave each purchaser a receipt and an autographed picture of herself with the message, "Thank you for joining with me in this vital crusade to make America strong." After a few exhausting hours in the jammed lobby, she had sold $2,017,531 worth of Defense Bonds and Stamps, quadruple what the goal had been.

That evening, as Carole appeared on stage at the Cadle Tabernacle, several thousand people filled the hall to hear her speak at another war bond rally. Three military bands and a color guard enhanced the patriotic event; flags hung from the ceiling, a huge banner declaring, "Sacrifice, Save and Serve." An all-Black chorus sang the "Lord's Prayer." Carole, clad in a strapless evening gown, joined the enthusiastic crowd in singing "The Star Spangled Banner." The three bands and a pipe organ provided a mighty accompaniment. It was a stirring event. The bond tour now concluded, Carole, her mother and Winkler began making plans to return to Hollywood.

Bessie and Winkler favored returning home by rail, but Carole said the trip out and the bond rally had been so exhausting that she couldn't bear three days on a train. Besides, she was quite anxious to return to Gable. They had apparently resolved their differences by long-distance telephone.

Bessie was concerned about flying that day. A strong believer in numerology and astrology, she warned Carole and Winkler that it was January 16 and that the number 16 was a warning of possible accident or death. Moreover, Bessie said, her astrologer had advised her just a few weeks before: "Stay off planes in 1942." Although Carole was also interested in astrology and usually followed her mother's advice, she insisted on returning home by airplane.

"When I get home," she said, "I'll flop into bed and sleep for 12 hours."

When they arrived at the Indianapolis airport, Bessie became further alarmed about flying that day because she learned that their flight number was 3 and that they would be flying on a DC-3. Furthermore, Carole was 33 years old.

Carole, Bessie and Otto Winkler boarded a Douglas DC-3 airliner. TWA Flight #3, leaving Indianapolis at 4:00 p.m., was scheduled to arrive in Burbank, California that night after stops in Albuquerque, New Mexico, and Las Vegas, Nevada.

Winkler wired Gable that the flight would arrive at 8:00 p.m. Gable instructed his servants to plan and prepare a marvelous homecoming dinner. Joining him and his wife would be Carole's brothers, Otto Winkler and his wife, Jill. Gay, fresh flowers were placed throughout the ranch home. As a gag, Gable put a store window mannequin under the sheets of

Gable played a suave jewel thief posing as a Lloyd's detective in They Met in Bombay *in 1941.*

Carole's bed. He grinned as he imagined her reaction at finding it there.

Carole, Bessie and Otto Winkler, on board the plane, settled in their seats. Carole began work on the script for her next film, *They All Kissed the Bride*, which would begin shooting shortly.

The airliner stopped in Wichita, where concert violinist Joseph Szigeti, a Hungarian refugee, boarded the flight. In Albuquerque, Szigeti and three other civilians were bumped from the flight because the transport was to be filled to capacity with airmen returning from the Army Ferrying Command to a base in California. A TWA employee asked Winkler if the Lombard party would relinquish their seats for three more Army men. Carole chose not to. She was allowed to make this refusal only because she was returning from a government war bond rally assignment.

Flight #3 usually flew nonstop from Albuquerque to Burbank. This time, however, it stopped in Las Vegas at 6:36 p.m. to be refueled and serviced. At 7:07 p.m., it took off for Burbank.

Larry Barbier, an MGM publicist, had been sent to Burbank Airport to meet the Lombard party. He was to call Gable as soon as he learned the exact arrival time. Gable had decided not to go to the airport, knowing that press photographers and reporters would be present to cover Carole's return, and he did not want to deprive her of well-deserved publicity.

Gable waited at the ranch. The call from Barbier did not come. Instead a call came from Eddie Mannix, an MGM official and one of Gable's closest friends. The call came at about the time the plane was due, so Gable figured the flight had arrived in Burbank.

"Carole's plane went down a few minutes after it left Vegas," Mannix said in a somber tone.

There was a pause.

"How bad is it?" Gable asked.

"We don't know yet, but we better get to Vegas right away."

Mannix quietly informed Gable that the studio had already chartered a plane and that MGM publicists Howard Strickling and Ralph Wheelwright would pick him up shortly and drive him to the airport. Gable hung up the phone and awaited their arrival.

En route to the airport, Gable, Strickling and Wheelwright listened attentively to the car radio. They learned that workers at the Blue Diamond Mine outside of Vegas reported hearing an explosion. Immediately following the explosion, they saw a brilliant light flaring in the skies shortly after 7:00 p.m.

When the trio finally arrived in Las Vegas, Gable learned that the wreckage had been spotted by a Western Airlines pilot. Two rescue parties consisting of sheriff's deputies, miners, ranchmen and army recruits had been organized. They had found the crash site: the 8,500-foot Doubleup Peak, 50 miles southwest of the Las Vegas airport. No roads led to the site and the existing trails were covered with snow. The location was virtually inaccessible. Although 100 people had joined the salvage group, only a select few, those in excellent physical condition, would continue past a camp near Good Springs, 35 miles southwest of Las Vegas.

Gable arrived in Las Vegas too late to join the first rescue team. He wanted to go with the second unit, but Mannix dissuaded him. He didn't want Clark to view the terrible scene.

Gable rented a private bungalow at the El Rancho Vegas Hotel. From his window he could see a reddish-orange light—probably the burning wreckage. Howard Strickling stayed with Gable. The movie star said little; he continuously paced the floor and chain-smoked cigarettes. Meanwhile, reporters and curiosity seekers gathered outside.

Before departing on their mission, the rescue party was informed that it would take approximately 24 hours to reach the crash site. The trip down the mountain side to the wreckage itself would be long and hard.

Several hours later, Gable received a telegram from Mannix and Wheelwright, who had gone to the scene of the crash: "NO SURVIVORS. ALL KILLED INSTANTLY." Gable was stunned.

The aircraft, seven miles off course, had crashed into a rock cliff several hundred feet below the crest of the mountain. It had split in half and burst into flames upon impact. The charred remains of the 22 passengers were scattered about.

Gable had hoped that a memento—a ring, a fragment of clothing, anything that was Carole's—would be found. An Army recruit did find a piece of one of the ruby and diamond clips Carole was wearing. He gave it to Gable. Gable would treasure it always.

Gable felt responsible for the deaths of Carole, her mother and Otto Winkler. "Perhaps if I had gone with Carole on this trip, all might have been avoided," he said.

Mannix and Wheelwright assured Gable that Carole did not suffer. The death had been instantaneous. "She never knew what happened," they said.

The trail to the crash site was very narrow and treacherous. It would be at least two or three days before the bodies could be brought down from the mountain peak.

Al Menasco and Buster Collier, another close friend, tried to comfort Gable during the grim wait. Clark drove with Menasco to the foot of the mountain. He talked earnestly to the searchers, expressing his gratitude and helping to serve food to the rescue team. He gave a deputy sheriff $100 when he saw a toothless rescue worker trying to eat a steak. "For God's sake, buy that guy some teeth," said Gable. Ironically, it was X-rays of Carole's teeth that helped in the identification of her body.

After a coroner's inquest, Gable, his friends, and MGM representatives accompanied the bodies of his wife, his mother-in-law and Winkler back to Los Angeles by train.

Carole Lombard was 33 years old and at the peak of her career when she died in a plane crash in January, 1942.

"I DO NOT want to go back to an empty house in Los Angeles," is Clark Gable's reply to friends who wait with him at El Rancho Vegas as rescue workers fight desolate terrain to reach the body of Miss Lombard. This picture of the famous couple was taken shortly after they had eloped to Kingman, Ariz.
—Picture from International News Photograph Service.

ALTHOUGH CAROLE LOMBARD is dead, the memory of a gay and beautiful girl will live in the hearts of her many friends and countless screen fans. This is Miss Lombard on the set of "To Be or Not to Be," her last film.

WHEN MISS LOMARD was 12 years old she appeared in her first picture, "The Perfect Crime," in which Monte Blue was the star. Only a few years later she was to star from the same studio in almost every type of role. Her greatest and best loved roles, however, were in light comedies, such as "My Man Godfrey."

"SHE GAVE HER life for her country's Flag." This high tribute has been given Miss Lombard by high Government officials. For the actress, pictured raising the Flag at Indianapolis, where she launched a gigantic Defense Bond and Stamp sales drive, was serving the United States when her plane crashed in Nevada.
—Picture from International News Photograph Service.

Aid in Search

Start Long Hike to Wreck

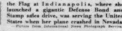

PIUTE INDIANS and desert hardened miners are helping to recover bodies of the plane's victims. The snow covered country is exceedingly difficult to traverse and it may be days before the tragic task is completed.

SOLDIERS AND civilians of a rescue party here are pictured starting the long climb to scene of the wreck high in the mountains just outside Las Vegas. Horses cannot be used so rough is the area of the disaster.

Newspapers devoted considerable attention to Carole Lombard's death in the crash of a TWA airliner into a Las Vegas mountain.

The death of Carole Lombard, age 33, saddened the nation. Will Hays, czar of the film industry, echoed the feelings of many mourners: "Carole Lombard has given her life in the service of America." America agreed.

President Roosevelt wired Gable: "Mrs. Roosevelt and I are deeply distressed. Carole was our friend, our guest in happier days. She brought great joy to all who knew her and to millions who knew her only as a great artist. She gave unselfishly of her time and talent to serve her government in peace and in war. She loved her country. She is and always will be a star, one we shall never forget nor cease to be grateful to. Deepest sympathy."

Carole was posthumously awarded a medal by Roosevelt. It read: "The first woman to be killed in action in the defense of her country in its war against the Axis powers."

The U.S. Senate paused to hear a tribute to Carole Lombard made by Senator Willis of Indiana. On January 19, 1942, at 12:00 noon, Hollywood film studios stopped all activities: taps was sounded in memory of a great film star.

Double funeral services—for Carole Lombard and her mother—were held on January 21 at the Church of Recessional, Forest Lawn Memorial Park. Carole's will dictated her funeral services. The public and photographers were barred; a few reporters were admitted; the 46 mourners in the chapel were either friends or relatives; only a few movie stars were invited—William Powell, Spencer Tracy, Myrna Loy, Fred MacMurray and Jack Benny.

Gardenias and orchids blanketed the closed coffins of Lombard and her mother. The only music came from an organ as a Methodist minister read from John 14: "Let not your heart be troubled." He then recited the 23rd Psalm, followed by a favorite poem of Carole and her mother. Friends added a tribute: "Only those are fit to live who do not fear to die, and none are fit to die who have shrunk from the joy and duty of life."

Services for Otto Winkler were conducted on the following day. Gable escorted Winkler's widow, Jill, to the funeral and promised that he would do everything possible to provide for her future.

When Gable returned to the ranch, Jean Garceau handed him a note Carole had written before she departed for the bond tour. As Jean stood by his side, Clark read the note. He broke down and cried bitterly. Until that time, Jean noted, "Clark had borne himself with fortitude and courage, had been stronger than any of us throughout the entire ordeal . . . After that Clark was in perfect control, his grief masked. He asked no sympathy, wanted none, was unapproachable."

Gable did not immediately return to the film he had begun shooting just before the crash. Ironically titled, *Somewhere I'll Find You*, MGM suspended production for a month. Accompanied by his hunting pal Harry

Fleischmann, Gable spent two weeks at the Rogue River in Oregon.

When it was time to resume work on the film, he refused to do so until the title was changed. MGM complied, renaming the picture *Red Light*. (When it was released in August, 1942, the original title was used.) On the set, Gable seemed his usual self, except for the fact that he was 20 pounds thinner, drank heavily and, whereas he formerly ate in the commissary with others, he now ate alone in his dressing room.

At home, Gable spent hours roaming the ranch alone. He watched Carole's films on the projector, looked through scrapbooks of their life together, and read or drank himself to sleep. His wanderings on the ranch inevitably took him to those places that evoked fond memories of his life with Carole—the orchards, the stables, the garden. He stared at the Dodge station wagon in the garage and, remembering their trips in it, never drove it again. Carole's dachshund, Commissioner, now followed Gable everywhere. Before her death, the dog never so much as approached him.

Gable ordered the servants to leave Carole's room untouched and unchanged. Except for the clothing she had purchased from her wardrobe in her last film, which was returned to United Artists for a refund, all of her belongings were left in their proper place.

Lombard's will left almost everything to Gable. Her assets, not including the ranch, were estimated at $300,000. Their home was in Gable's name despite the fact that she had originally paid for it. Carole left annuities to her friend "Fieldsie" Lang and to her mother, the latter subsequently divided equally between Carole's two brothers. Gable, who had never been close to the brothers before, refused to have anything to do with them after the funeral.

Several months after Carole's death, Gable considered selling the ranch. He looked at homes in Beverly Hills, Bel-Air and Brentwood, but decided to remain in the home he and Carole had enjoyed.

"For months after her death, Clark was almost out of his mind with grief," said writer Adela Rogers St. John, a close friend. "I'd go to his house and he'd be having dinner alone in the dining room with Carole's dog and Siamese cats near the table . . . I asked, 'Why don't you go out? Why don't you call your old friends like Vic Fleming?' And he'd say, 'Carole used to make the calls when we wanted to go out.' "

The release of Carole's last film, *To Be or Not to Be*, was delayed by United Artists until an appropriate mourning period had passed. A line of dialogue in which Carole asks Jack Benny, "What can happen in a plane?" was excised from the film.

Joan Crawford assumed the lead in what was to be Carole Lombard's next picture, *They All Kissed the Bride*. It was understood that her entire $112,500 salary would go to the Red Cross and other wartime charitable causes.

Crawford, who had been Gable's friend many years before, invited

Gable played a war correspondent in Somewhere I'll Find You. Here, he and Frank Faglen head for the firing lines of Bataan.

Lana Turner appeared with Gable in Somewhere I'll Find You, *the picture on which he was working when Carole Lombard met her tragic death.*

him to her home where they talked for hours. She bluntly told Clark that it was time to rid himself of the guilt he felt about Carole's death and that now that he had felt his grief he should push on to the next phase of his life. When the Gable-Crawford visits continued during the next four or five months, Hollywood gossips started speculating. Crawford explained that Gable was a "moody man who needed friendship." She reminded the whisperers that Gable had helped her through a troubled time in the early thirties.

Clark was constantly confronted with reminders of his late wife. The release of her last film resulted in many articles about her. A newly-recruited Indiana Naval Air squadron was named "The Lombardiers" in Carole's honor. *Carole Lombard's Life Story*, a souvenir magazine, appeared on the newsstands.

With *Somewhere I'll Find You* completed, Gable talked of joining the service. MGM, already having lost some of its younger stars to the draft, was trying to hold on to Gable. The studio offered to star him in a biography of Eddie Rickenbacker, the World War I flying ace and car racer. MGM said the film would be a splendid morale builder for the country. They tried to convince Gable that the film, in its own way, would help the war effort. Gable was unconvinced. He was becoming more and more serious about joining the Armed Forces. He would fulfill one of Carole's most fervent wishes.

7

Gable Joins the Air Force

IN THE SUMMER OF 1942, Clark Gable enlisted as a private in the United States Army.

"I don't want to sell bonds," he said. "I don't want to make speeches, and I don't want to entertain. I just want to be where the going is tough."

Gable's enlistment, though said by some to be his way of escaping from the sadness and loneliness that had engulfed him, was certainly a granting of Carole's last wish. There was another reason, as columnist Hedda Hopper later surmised. "Clark always yearned for the realities of life to compensate for his artificial existence as a movie star," she wrote. "It explains largely his hunting and fishing expeditions into the wilds, his ranch home. It was one reason why Clark had to go to war, even though he was overage."

Clark was earning $7,500 per week at MGM when, on August 12, 1942, he entered the service as a buck private—serial number 19125047—at $66 a month! He proved a good example for Hollywood and the nation. He was sent to Officers' Candidate School (OCS) near Miami, Florida. An Air Force colonel told him that the U.S. Army was having trouble recruiting enough aerial gunners, so he volunteered for aerial gunnery. The publicity that Gable was seeking wings as a gunner would in itself alleviate the shortage.

Before entering the service, Gable had made final preparations for the upkeep of his ranch. In unpublicized negotiations between Gable and MGM, the studio agreed to pay him $150,000 a year while he was in the service. In turn, MGM was granted an option on Gable's services after the war. MGM also made secret arrangements with the government to have Andy McIntyre, a studio camerman, inducted and assigned to the same base as Gable throughout his time in service. It was a gesture designed to help the actor adjust to military life.

At Officers' Candidate School, Gable suffered the same indignities as other recruits. His famous mustache was shaved; his hair was cut short. He was assigned the usual manual labor, such as scrubbing floors. But when he was assigned guard duty, it proved troublesome: as he walked along the perimeters of the base, women marched alongside him on the other side of the fence. They tossed him notes offering their phone numbers and propositions.

Gable also got his share of hazing, a common practice in OCS where officers often peppered new recruits with embarrassing questions. One officer, picking on him repeatedly, gave him demerits for not having his shiny brass belt buckle up to standards. (The officer would wet his thumb and run it across Clark's buckle.)

OCS training is tough enough for any young man, and Gable, at age 41, was forced to keep up with men half his age. When reveille was sounded at 4:15 a.m., the men had 15 minutes to ready themselves for fall-in. A march of a mile or two preceded breakfast. There were rigid exercise drills, including long distance running, to get the men in top physical condition.

As an OCS candidate, much classroom work and studying was required. Gable, who had been out of school for 25 years, and had never been a good student, was able to maintain good grades by memorizing class material as he would a movie script. Sometimes, when there was much to study, he spent the night in the latrine after the lights had been turned out in the barracks.

Gable neither asked for nor received any special consideration during his stay at OCS. He behaved like the other recruits, and they soon grew to like him. Once, he took out his upper denture in the washroom and waved it, laughing, "Look at the King, the King of Hollywood. Sure looks like the Jack now, doesn't he?"

While a cadet, Gable had to duck and dodge socially ambitious officers' wives who were always trying to snare him for cocktail or dinner parties. In answer to requests by the public and press photographers, the Air Force issued a press release: "Gable will appreciate it if the public will not interfere with his training. He wishes to be treated like every other member of the service."

Clark completed OCS in the upper third of his class, ranking 700th among 2,600 recruits. He was commissioned a second lieutenant, serial number 0-565390, on October 29, 1942 and was assigned to Gunnery School at Tyndall Field near Panama City, Florida. Granted a leave for Christmas, 1942, he decided to fly to Los Angeles. After a delay in Texas, where the airplane had engine trouble, he returned to the ranch. He saw only a few close friends, including actress Virginia Grey. Tanned, his

(Right) Lieutenant Clark Gable graduated from the Army Air Corps Officers' Candidate School near Miami, Florida on October 20, 1942. (Below) Gable manned a machine gun at the open waist window of a B-17 in a raid over Osnabruck, Germany in 1943.

mustache grown back, and having regained lost weight, he looked very handsome in his tailor-made officer's uniform. The five months in the service had given him a healthy, robust look. But inwardly, he remained very distraught about the death of his wife. Gable told his secretary, Jean Garceau, "You know, I have everything in the world anyone could want but one thing. All I really need and want is Ma." As a remembrance of Carole, he had the battered remains of her ruby and diamond clip fitted into a tiny gold case which he wore around his neck with his service tags.

Gable was home only a few days, but he managed to get quite a few business matters resolved with Jean. He inspected his ranch and was pleased with its upkeep during his absence.

Gable graduated from Gunnery School on January 7, 1943 and received silver wings, qualifying him to fly on high altitude bombers. He was immersed in several weeks of advanced gunnery training at Fort George Wright near Spokane, Washington when he was assigned by General "Hap" Arnold to produce films about aerial gunners. The Army would use these movies for the purpose of recruiting and training men. He traveled to several bases in the United States to gather information and assemble a film production crew.

Gable and the crew flew to England to work on the film. Upon arrival, he was assigned to the 351st Bomber Group, a heavy bombardment unit at the Peterborough Air Base, situated 80 miles from London. Gable, McIntyre and John Lee Mahin, an MGM scriptwriter, were promoted to cap-

Gable is pictured with the crew of the Delta Rebel in July, 1943, at an air base in England.

tain. The Air Force called it a routine promotion in the table of organization through openings created by heavy losses of men.

With Gable's arrival in England came numerous requests for appointments from war correspondents and photographers. The Air Force rejected all. Finally, under heavy pressure from reporters, a special day was set aside for Gable to meet the press. C. Carlton Brechler, now Western Region public relations manager for General Motors, was a captain handling Air Force public relations in England at the time. "Virtually every major newspaper, magazine and wire service was represented there," said Brechler. "Gable was friendly and posed for photographers and answered the reporters' questions." Most of the time was spent posing for newsreel and still photographers.

Looking over the insignia of the Delta Rebel No. 2 must have reminded Gable of Gone With the Wind, *a film which he had completed just three years earlier.*

Working with the photographic unit kept Gable busy. The unit filmed not only actual combat scenes, but scenes on the base showing both preparation for raids and relaxation between chores. Crews returning from battle were interviewed and photographed; so were combat casualties who were now hospitalized. Gable worked hard and passionately; he became very proud of the airmen at the base. "They are the greatest men in the world," he said in a radio interview, "and every one of them is doing a fine job, risking his life daily for us all."

Gable spent several months in England working on his film. The assignment involved him in five dangerous missions in which he doubled as a cameraman aboard B-17 Flying Fortresses. His first mission was a raid on Antwerp in May of 1943. Later, participating in a sortie into Germany aboard a B-17 called "Ain't It Gruesome?" he spent most of the 17-hour flight shooting pictures. As he stood with a small camera in his hand, wedged behind the top turret gunner, a 20mm shell penetrated the floor, ripping off the heel of Gable's boot. It just missed his ear and tore a hole in the fuselage a foot from his head. "After that Gable was really accepted as one of the boys," said Mahin.

Gable also raided a heavy water plant in Norway and a prime-target industrial center in Germany's Ruhr Valley. On another flight, he manned a gun at the open waist window in a raid over Osnabruck, Germany. In a mission over France, he took over the nose gun to help fight off enemy planes. After completing this mission, in October, 1943, he received the Air Medal for "exceptional meritorious achievement while participating in five separate combat bomber missions."

The Nazis, well aware of Gable's presence, offered a $5,000 reward, a promotion and furlough for his capture. Gable confided to friends that if his plane were ever shot down, he would go down with it. "How can I hide with this face?" He dreaded the thought of being captured by the Nazis who he was sure would exhibit him all over Germany like a side-show freak.

Although a captain, Gable never requested special treatment. He slept in a small, sparsely furnished room in the barracks with the other men. Because he was quite a bit older than most of them, they affectionately called him "Pappy."

He grew to love the men with whom he lived. When one who had been used as a subject in one of his films died on a mission, Gable took the time to write the man's widow a letter of condolence.

Gable returned from Europe by plane in late October, 1943, after shooting 50,000 feet of film. The film and camera equipment was shipped by boat. He reported to the Pentagon in Washington, D.C., where he learned that the War Department had arranged a press conference for him. Employees of the Pentagon jammed its corridors; scores of reporters waited in the conference room. Gable felt somewhat embarrassed at this "hero's welcome"—he knew other servicemen who had done so much more. Arriving in Pasadena, California by train a few days later, while on furlough, he was greeted by reporters, photographers and a crowd of about 300. Awaiting the arrival of his film, Clark enjoyed his Encino ranch and spent many happy hours working about the place.

Gable's homecoming was saddened, however, by the November 28th death of his close friend, Harry Fleischmann, who had been stricken by a heart attack. Gable drove to Bakersfield to attend the funeral.

While home, awaiting assignment orders from the War Department, Gable continued to enjoy the comforts of the ranch. He liked the quietness, especially when he recalled the tumult he had experienced in war-torn Europe. "I saw so much in the way of death and destruction, I realized that I hadn't been singled out for grief—that others were suffering and losing their loved ones just as I lost Ma," he confided in Jean Garceau.

The ranch, of course, brought back many memories of the happy days he had spent there with Carole. When he examined her room, he saw that everything had remained intact. It had been nearly two years since her death, and he still mourned her deeply; he felt lonely without her. During his evenings, he would often visit director Walter Lang and his wife "Fieldsie," who had been close friends of Carole and retained ties with Clark. He visited other friends and saw much of Virginia Grey.

Actress Virginia Grey continued to be one of Gable's favorite companions after he returned from military duty.

Gable, still awaiting his film from Washington, spent Christmas Day of 1943 with the Walter Langs. Early in 1944, as he began to transform the Air Force footage into training and educational movies, he was assigned to the Air Corps' photograph division headquarters at Hal Roach Studios in Culver City. Most of his time, however, was spent working on the training films using the more elaborate facilities of nearby MGM. When he paid his first visit to the MGM commissary, a huge crowd awarded him a standing ovation.

Gable chatted with Lieutenant James Stewart, another MGM star, while on leave early in 1943 before departing for England. Stewart became an Air Force pilot.

On January 15, 1944, he was guest of honor at the launching of the Liberty Ship, *S.S. Lombard*. The ceremony at the Terminal Island docks of the California Shipbuilding Corporation was a poignant assignment for Gable—15,000 people attended. Dressed in his Air Force uniform, Gable listened with his head bowed as Louis B. Mayer eulogized Carole Lombard. Gable, his fists clenched tightly, spoke briefly. He choked with emotion as actress Irene Dunne cracked a bottle of champagne against the ship. Gable, tears streaming down his cheeks, stood at attention and saluted.

After his return from military service, while awaiting work in films, Gable became a motorcycle enthusiast.

For the next five years, he continued to work on his Air Force training films for the War Department at MGM studios. It was a huge task which required editing some 50,000 feet of film and narration. Clark did the narration from a script written by MGM writer John Lee Mahin. Gable was shown only occasionally in the film. When finally completed, the footage produced five training and educational films.

Gable was promoted to the rank of major in May, 1944, just before being honorably discharged on June 12, 1944, and just before being placed on inactive status by the Army. Captain Ronald Reagan (the actor who two decades later was to become governor of California) of the Air Corps Personnel Office, Culver City, signed his discharge papers.

Immediately upon his release, MGM renewed its contract with Gable for another seven years at $7,500 a week. The new contract provided for four months of vacation and the right to stop work at 5:00 p.m. Gable, now 43, was beginning to show touches of grey at the temples, but MGM maintained its confidence in the handsome actor's power to reclaim his throne as a top box-office attraction.

Gable had been among the "top ten" at the box office for a decade of his 13 years as a motion picture actor. It was an achievement unmatched by any other star. Theaters in every country in the world ran Gable films. Unlike other handsome stars of the era—Tyrone Power, Robert Taylor, Robert Montgomery and Errol Flynn—he had combined the best qualities of such silent stars as Douglas Fairbanks and Rudolph Valentino. As far as MGM was concerned, Gable was still the "King of Hollywood."

In September, 1944, although officially no longer in the service, Gable traveled to Washington to deliver the finished prints of his training films to the War Department. In addition to their use for recruitment and training of Air Force personnel, the films were shown at bond rallies and war plants.

Gable's Washington business completed, and his next film not yet ready to go into production, he went to New York for a vacation. There, he dated Dolly O'Brien, a very wealthy, beautiful, blue-eyed, blonde socialite whom he had met years earlier through her former husband. She invited him to a party at her West Palm Beach, Florida home. He spent two weeks there and returned to his ranch in time for Christmas, spending it with MGM publicist Howard Strickling and his wife, who were among Gable's closest friends at the time.

Adjusting to civilian life was difficult for Gable. Al Menasco and some old friends were still in the service and he was left with much free time before beginning work on a film with MGM. He loved the calm of ranch life compared to the turmoil of war, but often was lonely. Gable spent quiet evenings at home—alone—or with a few close friends. One was Nan Fleischmann, widow of his friend Harry Fleischmann. He visited Nan often at her Pacific Palisades home. Clark also spent time with Eddie

Gable was discharged from the Air Force in the summer of 1944 and was promoted to major just before being placed on inactive status.

Mannix—when he was not tinkering with his cars.

Clark found a new hobby: riding motorcycles in the hills in the Calabasas area of the San Fernando Valley. He rode with actors Keenan Wynn, Ward Bond and Andy Devine and directors Howard Hawks, Victor Fleming and William Wellman. Studio executives were not pleased about these adventures; they feared for his safety. The movie star was undisturbed by their concern.

In 1945, Gable began to socialize more and more. Never a night clubber before, he became a frequent visitor of such night spots as Ciro's and the Mocambo. He could invariably be found with a beautiful girl at his side. Others swarmed after him.

Besides Virginia Grey, with whom he was seen now and then, he dated Kay Williams, a beautiful blonde, and Anita Colby, the famous model who had appeared on the covers of so many magazines and was consequently known as "the Face." Gable also spent time with Betty Chisholm, a widow who had a home in Phoenix in the Arizona Biltmore Estates. The two played golf and rode horses together.

Gable dated quite a few women, wandering from one to another, but none had yet won his heart. He had still not recovered from the loss of Carole, and his spirits were often low. This may have accounted for his drinking problem. For years, Gable had been liberal with his intake of scotch, but now he was imbibing a great deal—and very often.

8

Gable Marries a Lady

GABLE'S BACK AND GARSON'S GOT HIM! This announcement, splashed all over newspapers, magazines and billboards, was an advertising headline for *Adventure*, Gables's first picture after the war. Gable resented it. Not only had he been unhappy with the script, but he and Greer Garson, who had won the 1942 Academy Award for Best Actress for her work in *Mrs. Miniver*, didn't get along. *Photoplay's* review commented: "What we can't understand, however, is the vociferous and he-mannish Mr. Gable consenting to mouthe the innocuous and, at times, whimsical dialogue that means just nothing."

Despite *Adventure's* flaws, the picture, released on December 28, 1945, grossed close to $7 million. One thing was obvious: Gable's loyal fans were glad to see him back on the screen.

If Gable was unhappy with *Adventure*, he was more troubled by his personal life. Still not recovered from the loss of Carole Lombard, he drank more heavily. Usually, he could hold his liquor well without much effect, but one day the overdrinking nearly cost him his life.

Early one morning in 1945, while driving home from a night of partying, he lost control of his car and smashed into a tree off Sunset Boulevard at Bristol Circle in Brentwood. Fortunately for Gable, the crash occurred on property owned by Harry Friedman, vice-president of the Music Corporation of America. Friedman called MGM publicists who rushed to the scene, and luckily arrived before the police. They were able to keep the true story out of the newspapers by reporting that Gable had intentionally swerved his car to avoid a drunken driver. Gable was taken to Cedars of Lebanon Hospital. Though he had only suffered superficial cuts on his leg and face, he was kept hospitalized for several days . . . MGM wanted him to "dry out."

Advertising for Gable's return to the screen after military service played up the slogan "Gable's Back and Garson's Got Him!"

Gable's more active social life found him in the company of many beautiful women. He was still searching for another Carole Lombard. After finishing the filming of *Adventure*, he often visited the Gibson family lodge in Oregon and went fishing at the mouth of the Rogue River with Carol Gibson, the daughter of his good friends. She was a young, tall, slender, brunette sportswoman. Gable was fascinated by her, particularly her interest in the outdoor life, and they had much fun on their fishing trips together. But little came of the friendship, though Clark did see her again on later trips to Oregon.

From 1945 to 1948, Gable dated many types of women. He was seen with actresses Marilyn Maxwell, Paulette Goddard and Audrey Totter, with film producer Joan Harrison, and with waitresses and MGM secretaries.

He also continued to see Virginia Grey. They had dated each other frequently over the years in what could be called an "off-again-on-again" affair. "He'd go away for months and expect to come back and find me waiting," she later told reporters. "And I always was. Because I loved him. But, finally, one day I told him we were through."

Gable's free hours were not just spent pursuing lovely girls. He still enjoyed outdoor recreational activities and began playing golf again—usually with Eddie Mannix, with Howard Strickling of MGM, and with

Adolph Menjou. He renewed his membership at the Bel-Air Country Club where several other stars had become members. Gable grew to love golf, and he became quite good at it. In fact, one day, he achieved a hole-in-one on the 215-yard, 13th hole at Bel-Air.

In 1947, Gable, along with his actor friends Frank Morgan and Johnny Mack Brown, was cited for shooting 25 ducks during his two-day stay at a hunting lodge 10 miles south of Bakersfield. The legal limit was eight (four per day). Gable was summoned before Justice of the Peace Frank Norlega in Bakersfield and was fined $200. It was later revealed that Gable had been framed. The offense had really been committed by other members of the gun club.

Greer Garson and Gable in a scene from Adventure. *She played a librarian and he a tough, swaggering, romantic sea bos'n.*

Because of an eight-month union strike affecting all studios, Gable had not yet made a film in 1946. Gable had plenty of free time to pursue women and enjoy outdoor sports. MGM was still trying to find a good story in which to star him.

In 1947, Gable starred in a single film: *The Hucksters* with Deborah Kerr, Sydney Greenstreet, Adolph Menjou and Ava Gardner. Clark objected to the fact that the heroine in the story was an adulterous wife, so the screenplay version of the Frederic Wakeman novel was changed. The adulteress was made a genteel English widow; Clark played an advertising man. The movie, which told the behind-the-scenes story of Madison Avenue advertising agencies, was voted Best Picture of the Month by *Photoplay* magazine.

In the summer of 1947, one week after Dolly O'Brien divorced her fourth husband, Count Jose Dorelis, a Bulgarian-born perfume maker, she was seen in Hollywood with Gable. Their affair was brief. A somewhat longer relationship—one which lasted for several months—then developed between Gable and another beautiful socialite, Millicent H. Rogers, a three-time-married heiress to Standard Oil Company millions who lived on Long Island in New York. Both Dolly O'Brien and Millicent Rogers were women who lived in luxury and were socially active; they did not feel at home in Gable's outdoor sportsman world. And Gable had long ago decided—when he had been married to socialite Ria Langham—that he disliked the formal high society life.

Although not very active in film-making during this postwar period, Gable did not lose his considerable popularity with the public. One time, when appearing on NBC's *The Cavalcade of America* radio broadcast, he was mobbed by 350 women. DuPont, the sponsor, paid him a handsome sum, $7,500—50% more than most stars received—for playing a wartime submarine skipper. Radio dramas were not new to Clark. He had appeared in several Lux Radio Theater dramas in 1937.

Gable's next film, produced in 1948, was *Homecoming*, with Lana Turner and Ann Baxter, in which he depicted a successful New York society doctor who goes to war and becomes a major in the Medical Corps. His only other 1948 film was also a war story. In this picture, *Command Decision*, he played an Air Force general who ordered precision daylight bombing raids over Germany in World War II. Gable was pleased that all combat scenes in the movie were authentic.

Between the making of *Homecoming* and *Command Decision*, Gable decided to use some of the vacation-time owed him; and he made plans for a trip to Europe. On June 19, 1948, just before his scheduled departure, his stepmother, Edna, died. He delayed his trip to attend her quiet funeral at Hollywood Cemetery. A few weeks later he left for New York, from where he was due to sail on the *Queen Mary* on July 9. He arrived a few days before the ships's scheduled departure date and spent that time with Anita Colby.

Anita Colby, a cover girl model known as The Face, dated Gable often. Here, they attend a movie premiere in 1948.

Aboard ship, after a chance meeting, Clark's frequent dinner companion was actress Marilyn Maxwell, a beautiful blonde. The Howard Stricklings were in Europe on a business trip, and when Gable arrived there he spent some time with them. Howard scheduled a press conference for Gable in Paris and, when Gable learned that Katherine Hepburn was staying at the hotel, he asked her to join him at the confab. She did and they both kept very busy signing autographs for 350 members of the press.

Clark then began a motor tour of Europe. But when he received news that his father, age 78, had died on August 4, he had to cut short his vacation. Will Gable, he learned, was sitting in a chair reading a newspaper when stricken by a heart attack. He had died instantly.

On August 7, Clark, accompanied by the Stricklings, boarded the *Queen Mary* for the trip back to the United States. The funeral of Clark's father was delayed pending his arrival. Clark was quiet aboard ship and attended no shipboard activities.

Will Gable's funeral was a quiet one. Only Clark, Howard Strickling and Jean Garceau attended. Clark was, naturally, saddened by the death of his father, but he was consoled by the knowledge that he had helped make his father's last years comfortable.

Returning to work early in 1949, Gable found that Dore Schary, who replaced Louis B. Mayer as head of MGM, had cast him opposite Alexis Smith in *Any Number Can Play*. Most critics agreed that the script was weak, but Gable, playing an honest gambler, was wonderful. The picture was not a financial success.

With the picture completed, Clark took a four-month vacation. He spent a couple of weeks playing golf with Betty Chisholm at the Arizona Biltmore and, when he returned to Los Angeles, he dated Joan Harrison and Anita Colby. He also spent a great deal of time hunting and playing golf at Bel-Air Country Club. Meanwhile, MGM was still searching for some good stories for Gable's next films. There was visible evidence that a new trend was developing in film production.

Hollywood film studios, faced with rising labor costs and the imposition of a heavy tax on foreign film earnings, began trimming budgets in the late 1940s. Epics involving large casts and expensive sets were *out*; pictures emphasizing simple stories and realism were *in*. By 1949, employment at the studios had plummeted by about 25% from what it had been immediately after the war. Gable wanted parts in good, entertaining pictures and he was dissatisfied with the stories offered by MGM's Dore Schary. But he was under contract and the studio had the final word.

Although earning $7,500 a week, Gable was still plagued by a feeling of financial insecurity. He stashed his money where it was safe—in banks and in U.S. Savings Bonds. He always kept ready cash on hand, usually $500 to $1,000, and never carried a checkbook. Unlike many film stars, Clark did not invest in business or property. He shunned Las Vegas and, generally, restricted his gambling to a friendly card game with a 50-cent limit.

(Left) Gable, an avid golfer, makes a hole-in-one on the 215-yard, 13th hole at Bel-Air Country Club. (Right) Head professional, Joe Novak, of the Bel-Air Country Club, checks out Gable's golf game and gives him some pointers.

In another 1948 picture, Dark Decision, Gable portrayed a general who orders daylight bombing missions over Germany.

Spencer Tracy, Gable's friend and co-worker at MGM, visits Clark in his dressing room at the studio in 1949.

"When I got out of the Army, I was offered property all over the Valley," said Gable. "I was offered 100 acres for $100,000. Clarence Brown [a director] bought it, and sold it nine months later for $250,000." Gable's conservatism had lost him a golden opportunity to increase his fortune.

Gable's ranch home also reflected his frugality. It was actually quite modest compared to the modernistic facades of stone, steel and glass in which major film stars of the era lived. But this was of little importance to Gable. What troubled him most was that he had no one with whom to share his life. He was still looking for a woman who possessed the beauty, charm and warmth of Carole Lombard, and in December of 1949, he thought he met such a person. He became deeply involved with Lady Ashley, a beautiful, blue-eyed blonde who bore a great physical resemblance to Carole. Like Carole, she was amusing, witty, and liked to laugh. She was a well-mannered, sophisticated woman widely known in international cafe society.

Lady Ashley was born Sylvia Hawkes, daughter of a London pubkeeper and former stablehand. Sylvia was a dressmaker's mannequin and played in the musical comedy chorus of London's *Midnight Follies*. She was introduced by the Prince of Wales to Lord Ashley, heir to the Earl of Shaftesbury. Sylvia married Ashley in 1927.

In 1934, Ashley filed suit for divorce. A sensational court battle ensued in which Douglas Fairbanks was named as co-respondent. As soon as the divorce became final, Lady Ashley did indeed marry Fairbanks and, when he died in 1939, she received $1,000,000 of Fairbanks' $2,318,651 estate. In 1944, she married another British man of royalty, Lord Edward John Baron Stanley of Alderly. They were divorced in London in 1948 and she re-assumed the name of her first husband, Ashley. Returning to California, she lived in the Santa Monica beach home she had shared with Fairbanks, and became active in southern California's social scene.

Gable dated Sylvia many times in the fall of 1949, but not even his close friends suspected a serious involvement. They knew that while Clark saw much of Sylvia, he was also dating Betty Chisholm, Joan Harrison and, from time to time, several other women.

Gable, single for almost seven years, proposed to Sylvia Ashley on December 17, 1949, after having attended a party at the home of Charles Feldman. On their way home, at 2:30 a.m., Clark asked Sylvia for her hand in marriage. Their first public appearance together had been made at a party just three months earlier.

As with his marriage to Lombard, Clark decided on a quiet elopement. A formal wedding would have eclipsed any Hollywood ceremony for glamour and brilliance, but they chose simple rites. On December 20, 1949, they got a license in San Luis Obispo and were married in Solvang in a Danish Lutheran Church, 30 miles north of Santa Barbara. Mrs. Vera Bleck, sister of the bride, was matron of honor; Vera's husband, Basil, gave the bride away; Howard Strickling was best man. Also present were

Mr. and Mrs. Lynn Gilham, owners of the Alisal ranch in Solvang, where the reception was to be held, and Gable's secretary Jean Garceau. Guests at the wedding reception at the Alisal ranch included some of the dude ranch hands, invited inside for a drink. Recorded western music played on a phonograph.

When they returned to Los Angeles, the Gables met the press at the Encino ranch. They posed for pictures, and neither said much. The only time they stopped smiling was when a zealous female reporter asked the bride, "What was your recipe for getting Gable?" The couple found this question in poor taste.

Off to a two-week Hawaiian honeymoon, 400 well-wishers jammed the passageways and decks of the *Lurline* in San Francisco. They spent Christmas at sea.

They were greeted by several thousand people on their arrival in Honolulu. Aboard ship, Clark and Sylvia enjoyed the comforts of a suite which included two bedrooms, a sitting room, and a private deck. Meanwhile, Howard Strickling and his wife, Gail, had flown ahead to Honolulu and rented a house with a private beach for the newlyweds. In Hawaii, Clark played a good deal of golf. Sylvia walked or rode around the course with him. The Stricklings joined them in sunning on the beach and in boat rides. The Gables returned on the *Lurline* two weeks later.

Back in Los Angeles, they told the press of their great desire to have children. They were not a young couple: Gable was soon to be 49 and Sylvia, who had given her age as 39 at the time of the wedding, was reportedly 42.

Clark and Sylvia settled down at the Encino ranch. Their home life got off to a bad start. She wanted to fire Clark's black helper, a man of all trades, and install an English butler; Clark refused. She wanted to move to Beverly Hills or Bel-Air to be near society friends; he preferred the ranch. She wanted a personal maid, but Gable declined, saying that she was capable of drawing her own bath water. She spent an impressive amount of money on redecorating the home, smothering its masculine appearance with a frilly look. Sylvia enjoyed a life of parties, but Gable still liked the simple, informal home life with a few close friends dropping in. He disliked the frequent visits of her relatives, nor did he care for the lap dog she would ask him to hold. Clark's privacy had been intruded upon.

When Gable took Sylvia to a remote area of the Colorado rockies where he was filming *Across the Wide Missouri*, they lived in a secluded two-room cabin. She wanted to transform the cabin and its immediate environment into a more modern setting. It soon became obvious to Clark that Sylvia Ashley was not an outdoor girl. At the beginning of their stay in Colorado, she cooked in the cabin, but soon they ate in the mammoth

(Left) Sylvia Ashley, Gable's third wife, accompanied him to the Colorado Rockies when on location for *Across the Wide Missouri.* (Below) Sylvia Ashley borrows part of the Los Angeles Herald-Express *from Clark in their Colorado cabin.*

tent set up as the dining hall commissary for the entire company of 325 actors and technicians.

The Gable-Sylvia Ashley marriage lasted less than a year-and-a-half. It was common knowledge that the union was a mistake. First news of their separation came in April, 1951 when he went to Arizona to do "practice riding" for a new picture. She did not accompany him.

In June, shortly before she went to Nassau for a vacation, she filed for divorce, charging grievous mental cruelty. Gable filed a denial in which he declared that "she has no right to alimony . . . she is a millionaire," and is not entitled to community property, since all community funds acquired during their marriage had been spent or pledged on community debts.

When she made no move to expedite divorce papers, Gable moved to Nevada in October. He stayed at the Cal-Neva Lodge in the Lake Tahoe area and filed action in Las Vegas for a "quickie" divorce. During this period, he spent much of his time alone—swimming, hiking, riding, and playing tennis and golf.

The Nevada action tested a new California law which didn't recognize divorces granted in other states if the complainant had not been a California resident for the previous 12 months. On November 1, 1951, Superior Judge Orlando Rhodes ruled in Santa Monica that Gable couldn't get a Nevada divorce because he had filed an earlier answer in California.

Sylvia retained Hollywood attorney Jerry Geisler, who had a reputation for winning big settlements. Rumor had it that she sought $100,000 a year, up to a million dollars in all. Gable's attorney, W.I. Gilbert, found that "her demands for alimony were so unreasonable and exorbitant, it was obvious no agreement could be reached."

Sylvia, appearing in court on crutches due to a broken ankle sustained in a car crash, testified that Gable told her, "I want to be free. I don't want to be married to you or anyone else, and I want you to divorce me . . . There is no explanation. You have done nothing wrong. In fact, you have been quite wonderful. I am just not happy being a married man." She said he scarcely spoke to her after that. Rufus B. Martin, Gable's butler and handyman of 14 years, confirmed her story. "After dinner at night he would go directly upstairs to his room," said Martin. "Mrs. Gable would sit alone at the TV. He wouldn't talk to her. He was moody."

Sylvia added: "I tried everything I knew to get him to change his mind, to hold our marriage together. I ultimately had to give in."

Sylvia's friends said that she felt like a second wife; that she shared the house with Carole Lombard's memory. And Sylvia claimed that Gable never gave her any presents during the marriage, except a diamond necklace for her dog.

Judge Stanley Mosk granted Sylvia Ashley an uncontested, interlocutory decree on April 21, 1952. The 11-page property settlement awarded her $6,002.47 in cash, plus 10% of Gable's $500,000-a-year salary

Marilyn Maxwell, who appeared with Gable in Key to the City *in 1950, was one of the women he dated off-screen.*

and any radio and television income for the first year, and 7% for the next four years.

"I never understood Clark's marriage to Sylvia Ashley, whose pattern of life was so different than his," wrote columnist Louella Parsons. "I knew Sylvia well and, in justice to her, she was in love with Clark and felt that being married to him would give her some of the status and happiness that was hers when she was Mrs. Douglas Fairbanks."

"It was my pleasure to work closely with Clark Gable at the time of his marriage to Lady Ashley," said Howard Strickling. "Sylvia and Clark were attracted to each other and had a friendship before their marriage; however, their ways of life were entirely different and they were unable to adjust to marriage situations."

Gable, now 51, was once again a free man. His secretary, Jean Garceau, described him as "restless, bored and definitely at loose ends."

9
Happiness with Kay

GABLE'S DIVORCE FROM SYLVIA ASHLEY drained his finances. Again worried about financial security, he arranged to make his next three pictures abroad over an 18-month period. His salary would then not be subject to United States income taxes.

After making *Lone Star,* a western filmed in 1952 in the United States and co-starring Ava Gardner and Broderick Crawford, Gable appeared in *Never Let Go,* a film made in England. In it, he played a foreign correspondent who falls in love with a ballet dancer, played by Gene Tierney.

During the filming of the picture, which began shooting in mid-June, 1952, Gable was kept busy by 27-year-old, tall, slender Suzanne Dadolle d'Abadie. She was Schiaparelli's star mannikin model in Paris and had met Gable at a Paris cocktail party. The couple spent time together on the French Riviera, in Italy, boating on the Seine and frequenting the elegant Paris night clubs.

Gossip columnists wrote that Suzanne was "taming" Gable. He now was seen doing things that he had previously disliked: going to museums, operas and recitals. Clark reportedly telephoned her daily while away on location. "I'm a discreet woman, and I think that's what he appreciates," said Suzanne. "We have the same tastes and the same ideas. . . . We both like quietness and simple food." Wearing a huge topaz ring, a gift from Gable, she claimed engagement, but Gable denied it. Nothing became of their involvement. It was another one of Gable's brief affairs.

His next picture, *Mogambo,* found Gable cast again opposite Ava Gardner. *Mogambo,* a remake of *Red Dust* in which Gable had starred with Jean Harlow, began filming on location in Africa in the fall of 1952. Gossipers churned up a romance between Gable and Gardner, then

Ava Gardner, Gable and Grace Kelly starred in Mogambo, *a remake of* Red Dust, *which was filmed in Africa.*

married to Frank Sinatra. When Sinatra joined her on location, romance talk soon shifted. This time, it revolved about Gable and Grace Kelly, a beautiful 23-year-old blonde playing the second female lead in the film. She and Gable had become quite friendly, and they went on hunting expeditions together. Grace's beauty and her interest in hunting no doubt reminded Gable of Carole Lombard. But their age difference (Gable was 28 years older than Grace) was said to have presented difficulty. Other reports said Grace couldn't get used to Clark's false teeth. In any case, after his divorce from Ashley, Gable had vowed never to remarry.

After *Mogambo,* which was to become one of the big money-makers for MGM during the 1950s, Gable starred in *Betrayed.* In the film, shot in Holland and London, Gable played a Dutch intelligence officer who was rescued from the Germans and helped to find his way to England by a resistance leader, portrayed by Victor Mature. Lana Turner was the film's female star, and *Time* magazine said that Gable, at 53, "still has the he-manliest hug in the business." *Newsweek* called *Betrayed* a "clumsy and overslow pace piece of melodrama."

Betrayed, completed in London in December of 1953, was Gable's last MGM picture. His $7,500-a-week contract, up for renewal in the spring of 1954, was terminated by MGM. Some Gable biographers have claimed that MGM couldn't afford Gable's big salary. However, Howard Strickling, then an MGM vice-president said: "Gable was anxious to have his contract expire so he could free-lance. MGM would have gladly renewed but Gable was determined to strike out on his own." MGM had even flown

Lana Turner was Clark's love interest in Betrayed in 1954, his last picture for MGM.

Eddie Mannix to London to try to get Gable to renew his contract, but to no avail.

The decided trend to reduce film production costs by the studios was continuing. Television was already attracting many fans, and stars were now mostly being retained on a picture-by-picture basis.

Gable's split with MGM—legally, with Loew's Inc.—came after 23 years and more than 50 films. Gable's formal farewell statement read: "I want to avail myself of the opportunity of entering the free-lance field. I want to express my great appreciation to my many friends and associates at Loew's whose help I have had, and with whom I have had the pleasure of working. I wish also to pay tribute to my friends and associates who are no longer alive, and whose help and guidance over the years meant so much to me."

Gable was now relatively free of financial worries. He had been a member of MGM's pension plan for many years and had the option of drawing $31,000 a year for life, or collecting a lump sum in the amount of $400,000.

As a free-lancer, he announced, "I'm going to scout stories myself. I want good stories *without* a message. One of the main reasons pictures are better now is that producers have gotten back to the basic theory of entertainment. People don't want to be preached to. I'll never make a picture with a message."

Gable pondered his future. Some friends advised him to form a production company of his own, or to become a director. Others suggested retirement. At age 53, thanks in part to the success of *Mogambo* in 1954, he was still in the "top ten" at the box office. Studios were bidding for his services. While evaluating various offers, he met with friends whom he hadn't seen for a while because he had spent most of 1952 and all of 1953 in Europe.

When not thinking about his career, Gable enjoyed himself. He vacationed with Betty Chisholm in Phoenix for several weeks. They went horseback riding, played golf; and, when they returned to California, they went fishing with the Stricklings off Newport. Gable also continued to see Joan Harrison. He took her and the Stricklings on a fishing trip to Guaymas in Mexico.

Meanwhile, his agent, George Chasin of MCA, submitted several scripts to Clark. He disliked them all, except for *Soldier of Fortune*. Chasin negotiated a contract and, three months after his departure from MGM, Gable signed with Twentieth Century-Fox to do *Soldier of Fortune* with Susan Hayward. He played an American soldier of fortune who runs a profitable smuggling business on each side of the bamboo curtain. Many of the scenes in this CinemaScope film would be shot on authentic locations in Hong Kong. The film, which started shooting in the fall of 1954, was the first of a two-picture contract with Fox. Gable was to receive 10% of the box office gross, and expected a guarantee of about $500,000. As a free-lancer, on a percentage basis, he could choose his film roles more carefully, appear in fewer pictures, and earn more money than he did while under contract to MGM.

Gable was not doing as well in his personal life: he seemed to be withdrawing once again. He frequented night clubs less often—and then only at the studio's urging. When he was seen dancing with Marilyn Monroe in a night club in the fall of 1954, it sparked gossip. Gable was furious. He firmly refused to ever enter a night club again because romance rumors were the inevitable result.

Opening his morning mail, Gable strolls from the Raphael Hotel, where he lived during his stay in Paris in 1953.

Although Gable had been linked with as many women as was Errol Flynn, he was never involved in a scandal. Lew Smith, Gable's stand-in for many years, said in 1955: "I've seen him go through several phases in 20 years, but I've never seen him quarrel with or abuse anyone, or take out his troubles on someone else." People, whose lives Gable touched, respected him. Ex-girl friends made no trouble for him, nor did those with whom he had brief encounters.

In the fall of 1954, *Confidential,* a scandal magazine, tried to dig up some "dirt" on Gable and his former wives. It charged that he had used Josephine Dillon to further his career and that she was now a woman nearing her seventies, "living in near poverty." She was pictured as residing in an "old barn" while Gable roared down Ventura Boulevard, close by, in an expensive car. This was clearly not the case. The one-bedroom home had a spacious living room, a comparatively large kitchen, a big backyard, and was located in a fine area.

In 1955, Gable, out of definite gratitude, and possible guilt, purchased the home Josephine lived in at 12746 Landale Street in North Hollywood. He had it painted and repaired, then leased it back to her rent-free for the rest of her life.

Josephine, who had never remarried, remained dedicated to her drama teaching. In 1940, she wrote a book, *Modern Acting,* published by Prentice-Hall. Only rarely did she consent to interviews, and when she did she refused to say anything derogatory about Gable.

While Gable was bothered by the stories written about him in the scandal magazines, in 1955 he started to give interviews freely, something he hadn't done at MGM. "I haven't changed—MGM didn't want me interviewed," he told reporters. Now, as a free-lancer, he knew he could reap publicity which might contribute to the success of his films. He would also be able to set the record straight on several matters. Gable took advantage of the opportunity, but still remained reticent when it came to discussing details of his love life.

Gable, who turned down $100,000 from a publisher for his life story, told one interviewer, "I'm not rich by any means. But I'm comfortable. That's all I ask of life—to be warm, well fed and comfortable."

Asked about friends, he said, "I don't have a lot of friends. I do have a lot of acquaintances. Friends are something else."

In one interview, Gable exploded the persistent myth that he had undergone surgery to pin back his ears. He said he never had such an operation. His ears stuck out more in his younger days, he explained, because at that time he weighed considerably less and his face wasn't as full.

Clark refused to appear on television shows; he did not want to compete with the movie industry, and felt that it would be an act of disloyalty for him to appear on television. Whenever television aired old Gable films, the star's fan mail bulged with letters from people between the ages of 16 and 30 who were discovering the Gable their parents loved. "Maybe I'm indebted to television, but I never watch my old films on TV," he said. "It really burns me up competing with myself on two media." He did admit, however, that he generally enjoyed watching television—particularly boxing, wrestling and other sports.

After completing *Soldier of Fortune* early in 1955, Gable had some free time. He was waiting for location shooting to begin—in the spring of 1955 at Durango, Mexico—on *The Tall Men,* a post-Civil War western. Gable prepared for the role by practicing riding and roping at stables in Palm Springs. He had been drinking heavily since his divorce from Sylvia, had gained weight, and now put himself through a rigorous exercise program at the Encino ranch.

"I used to see him jogging every day along his horse pad area and bicycling," said Harry Maret, a movie studio make-up artist, who was then building a house near the Gable ranch. "I was just beginning construction of my home, and one day he came up the hill and we got acquainted. He started coming by every day and, one day, he volunteered to help me by taking care of coordinating the many construction details of the home, telling me that I didn't have to run back and forth from the studio to discuss matters with subcontractors. He said he'd be glad to take care of it for me. That's what I call a friendly neighbor!

The Tall Men, *co-starring Jane Russell and Robert Ryan, was one of two pictures Gable made for Twentieth Century-Fox for 10% of the box-office gross.*

"At the studio, people would ask me how my home was coming along and I'd say, 'Fine, I've got a good man taking care of the details for me.' If I told them he was Clark Gable, they wouldn't believe me. Gable was one of the few movie stars that I met in my 30 years in the make-up business who impressed me more when I met him in person."

The Tall Men, also starring Jane Russell, Robert Ryan and Cameron Mitchell, saw Gable play a Texan who had been an opponent of the Confederacy in the Civil War and then rode north to the gold fields of Montana to recoup his lost fortune. The breath-taking outdoor scenery and Gable's acting were praised in most reviews. The picture was a financial success.

Gable had now made two "free-lance" films, both of which were profitable. Gable had proven that his fans were loyal. But neither movie did much to satisfy Gable's desire to act a strong role in a good film. What would he do next? Gable wondered.

Gable also confronted another question: would he ever find the woman to replace Carole Lombard? He had dated many women since her death. One, who remained anonymous, was often quoted in newspaper articles regarding Clark's requirements for the ideal girl:

"In the evening he wants you to be better groomed and better mannered than anyone else at 21 or Le Pavillon or the Colony. And yet he hates to put on airs. He likes you to know how to use a swear word when the occasion calls for it. This ideal girl of his must also ride a motorcycle at 90 mph, rough it on a camping trip, cook a meal outdoors, clean out a chicken coop, weed a garden, and take four or five stiff drinks without getting giddy. Gable doesn't want much, does he?"

Many women had other thoughts about Gable. They described him as a man who was a realist and, yet, a romantic. They appreciated his awareness of a woman, and the attention he paid her, right down to noticing every detail of her appearance. He made a woman feel that he was interested in her both as a female and as a person. He dressed exceedingly well himself, and was a man of great dignity. Few women, if any, could resist him.

In the summer of 1955, Clark Gable married for the fifth time. Kay (Kathleen) Williams Spreckels, a 37-year-old, blue-eyed, blonde beauty and Gable, 54, were married on July 11. The ceremony took place in Minden, Nevada, 45 miles south of Reno, in Justice of the Peace G. Walter Fisher's yellow stucco cottage. With them were Mr. and Mrs. Al Menasco and the bride's sister, Mrs. Elizabeth Nasser of Beverly Hills. Clark and Kay spent a week's honeymooon at the Menasco ranch in St. Helena, California.

Gable had known the former model and actress for nearly 15 years. They dated frequently after his return from the service. When he went on a trip in the summer of 1945, she drove him to the airport, kissed him good-bye, and didn't hear from him for years. Nor did she make any attempt to contact him. She knew that he still had not recovered from the Carole Lombard tragedy.

Besides, Kay had just ended an eleven-month marriage to her second husband, Argentine cattle-king Martin de Alyaga Unzue, a lavish spender well known among the international set. Her first marriage to Parker Capps had been brief, too.

She was a teen-ager then. In September of 1945, she married Adolph B. Spreckels, Jr., heir to the Spreckels sugar fortune. They were divorced in July of 1952. She had two children with Spreckels—a boy, Adolph III (nicknamed "Bunker"), and a girl, Joan. Kay was reportedly worth $500,000 when she married Gable.

In Kay, Clark found a woman who could dress and look beautiful at public affairs and be just as happy hunting, fishing or playing golf. In her, he had found, at last, the chic elegance and tomboyishness that epitomized Carole Lombard. Kay, who had grown up on a farm in Erie, Pennsylvania, felt very much at home on the Gable ranch.

Gable's friends agreed that Kay possessed qualities similar to those of Carole. She (Kay) had made an unsuccessful attempt at a film career, but the experience gave her a knowledge of the film industry which helped her to understand her new husband.

At Kay's divorce trial from Spreckels, she had been accused by Spreckels of bringing Gable to their home after a party given by Jack Benny. Friends countered that Gable was at the party with Mr. and Mrs. Walter Lang and the three of them drove Kay home. Although Gable had many affairs in Hollywood, it was common knowledge that he would not get involved with a married woman. He was even known to have turned down dates arranged by friends if he learned that the woman was married.

In 1955, Clark and his wife, Kay, attended the premiere of The Tall Men, a CinemaScope picture with breathtaking outdoor scenery.

Despite Spreckel's attempt to defame Gable, the marriage between the movie star and Kay got off to a good start. Returning to the Gable ranch after their honeymoon, Clark informed Kay that he would agree to live wherever she chose. They could sell the ranch and buy a house in Bel-Air or Beverly Hills. But Kay loved the ranch. Furthermore, she felt it was an ideal place to rear her two children, then five and four years old. A new wing was added to make room for Bunker and Joan.

Gable found considerable joy in the children. He taught the boy how to ride horseback and both children how to swim in the swimming pool that had been installed at the ranch. He became very close with the children and they adored him.

Clark and Kay yearned for a third child. They were both disappointed when she had a miscarriage in her tenth week of pregnancy on November 3, 1955, following a bout with the flu.

Clark and Kay had been married less than a year when she was admitted to Cedars of Lebanon Hospital on June 13, 1956, having suffered a slight heart attack. He occupied a room next to hers for three weeks and even had some checkups himself. Kay convalesced in their home and made a good recovery.

At the ranch, Kay keyed her life to Clark's needs, much as Carole Lombard had done. She tagged along on his hunting and fishing trips. She learned how to shoot a gun and how to play golf. She respected Gable's memory of Lombard and preserved the atmosphere of the ranch.

"Kay made up her mind to be part of Clark's life," said Howard Strickling, who remained a close friend of Gable. "Whatever Clark wanted to do was fine with Kay. She was more than a wife. She was Clark's favorite companion and friend."

"There was genuine communication between us," said Kay. "We didn't play silly games like trying to make each other jealous."

Kay rarely visited her husband at the studio. After all, she explained, if she were married to a banker, would she pop into the bank? Gable seldom brought home problems he encountered at the studio. And when he did discuss business matters, she never offered advice.

Gable's screen popularity continued, dispelling any thoughts he may have had of early retirement. In a nation-wide poll of women, he was named the "most popular male star of 1955."

The screen magic of Gable—at the age of 54—was still very much alive. More and more studios and independent producers bid for his services. He was showered with scripts to read. But Gable now decided to form his own production company, Gabco. This would yield him a larger percentage of the gross.

The first film produced by Gabco was *The King and Four Queens* in which Gable played opposite Eleanor Parker and Jo Van Fleet. Released by United Artists in December of 1956, it was a romantic western with mystery and comedy. His acting once again received favorable reviews, but the picture did poorly. His experience with *The King and Four Queens* prompted Clark to disband the production company and work free-lance once again. He did so in 1957, after receiving an attractive offer from Warner Brothers to do a film at a salary of 10% of the gross. From that point on, Gabco became inactive.

In the film he made for Warner, *Band of Angels,* Clark played a reformed slave trader who maintains a plantation outside New Orleans. At a slave mart, he buys a well-bred white girl, played by Yvonne de Carlo. He treats her like a lady, and they fall in love. Reviews of the film and Gable's perfomance were mixed.

The year 1957 marked Gable's silver anniversary as a screen star. He was duly honored in the Congressional Record by Representative Wayne L. Hays, a Democrat from Clark's home state of Ohio. The tribute read:

> After a quarter of a century, Mr. Gable still reigns unchallenged as one of the world's most popular and best known movie personalities. . . . Time cannot wither, nor custom stale, Gable's infinite appeal. Mr. Clark Gable recently completed his 56th starring role. In his lengthy career, Mr. Gable contributed much to the enjoyment of millions. And at all times he was ready to fight for the principles which have made this country great.

Noting that Gable was born in humble circumstances, Representative Hays added: "He is the example of how a young American lad can advance himself and become famous."

Famous and rich as he was, Gable lived a quiet, simple life with Kay. When the Gables entertained, it was usually just a small circle of friends— the Gary Coopers, the Howard Stricklings, the Ward Bonds, the Al Menascos, Eddie Mannix—and a few others who were invited. The Gables also visited the homes of their friends.

Sometimes the couple went trapshooting at a gun club, or played golf. Gable also enjoyed romping with the children in the yard. The "King of Hollywood" threw fly balls and grounders to Bunker to help the youngster sharpen his baseball game, attended the boy's Little League games, and attended 4-H Club meetings. In the evening, Clark and Kay relaxed in the den and watched television. Only after much prodding would Gable run one of his old movies.

"It's fun raising youngsters at this stage in my life," Gable said. "Everything is new to them. Seeing things through their eyes gives me a fresh outlook on life, too. I couldn't be more pleased."

He also participated in the children's Halloween fun. He would show up at Encino Park with Kay, Bunker and Joan. One year, he disguised himself as a tramp, another as a clown.

Occasionally, Gable drove his Jeep along Ventura Boulevard, Encino's main street, to do some shopping. Passersby who noticed him rarely asked for his autograph. The Encino neighbors didn't want to intrude on his privacy. If he were spotted while driving to or from the studio, Gable would acknowledge his admirers with a smile and a wave of the hand.

Through the years, tourists continued to drive past the ranch, staring at it as they rode. Some even parked their cars, perched themselves in the hills and ate their lunches, waiting hopefully for even a glimpse of Gable.

In 1958, Gable co-starred with Burt Lancaster in *Run Silent, Run Deep,* a film in which he played a submarine commander. Gable, Lancaster and the film received good reviews. Another 1958 release was *Teacher's Pet,* in which he portrayed a self-taught city editor who becomes involved with a university professor (Doris Day). Gable went on tour to promote the film and stopped in Washington, D.C. to meet President Dwight D. Eisenhower.

In 1959, at the age of 58, Gable announced to the press that he now wanted to play roles appropriate to his age. "I do not want to play the young lover on the screen who sweeps starry-eyed maidens off their feet. I want to play roles appropriate to my age. I want to work because I love acting, and it's the only job I know, and I'm going to accept motion pictures in which I play an older man."

In another interview, he said, "I've spent a lot of time learning to be an actor. I'm still learning. I don't know how you go about learning to be a personality, but I do know how you learn to go about being an actor, and I work at it. It's a profession I'm proud of." Gable was always known to study his lines and the characters he was portraying diligently.

Doris Day played a university professor and Gable a self-taught city editor in Teacher's Pet, *a Paramount picture.*

In each of his next two films, Gable did exactly what he had stated: he played roles closer in age to his own. In *But Not for Me*, a comedy with Carroll Baker, Lili Palmer and Lee J. Cobb, he was an aging Broadway producer. He followed it with *It Started in Naples*, a comedy filmed in Italy with Sophia Loren, in which he was cast as a Philadelphia lawyer who arrives in Naples to settle the estate of his philandering brother. Kay and the children went with him to Italy.

Between *But Not for Me* and *It Started in Naples*, Gable had several months free. Besides hunting, fishing and working on the ranch, he spent much time in Palm Springs playing golf. In the late fall of 1959, he had a new home built off the sixth fairway of the new Bermuda Dunes Country Club. The $125,000 home boasted a large sunken living room with a high-beam ceiling, a den with an office, a guest room, and three bedrooms. The U-shaped house was centered around a swimming pool. Clark and Kay spent considerable time enjoying their new home and the clear, smogless desert air of Palm Springs. They also took golf more seriously at Bermuda Dunes. They bought golf books and read everything they could about the game.

"Gable worked out on the practice tee quite a bit," said Ed Vines, then head professional at Bermuda Dunes. "He also used to practice some short shots from the fairway at his home. He played every day and improved his game to the point that he was shooting in the high 70s or low 80s. He had a seven or eight handicap. His best score was a 73. He could hit the ball about 220 or 225 yards, but was not a good putter. He was a steady player, usually consistent, and hit a lot of greens in regulation."

"Gable and I played a lot of golf at Bermuda Dunes," said Ernie Dunlevie, who had become a Gable buddy after they had met in 1958 when Dunlevie was a film extra. Dunlevie, now a principal in the Bermuda Dunes Development Co., had an office in the clubhouse of the country club. Sometimes Gable played with some grape farmers from the area, and often he played with Kay. "He became one of the regulars at the club and would sit around and talk in the coffee shop and clubhouse bar with members of the club," Dunlevie recalled.

"Gable was not a great party guy. He liked a few close friends around and enjoyed having people over for dinner or go to somebody's house for dinner. I remember there were only six of us at a quiet party he had in his home for his 59th birthday [February 1, 1960]."

Dunlevie remembered how Gable had spent months at a time in Palm Springs enjoying his vacations. "He rode horses at Smoke Tree stables and we would attend the auto races at Riverside. He liked driving at high speed himself, and sometimes would speed along a lonely desert road in his gull-wing Mercedes 300SL. Gable wasn't a show-off with money, nor was he tight with it. He was a good check grabber—waiters usually gave him the check anyway. He was very thoughtful, always buying gifts for friends and

Gable played a reluctantly aging Broadway producer in But Not For Me *with Lee J. Cobb. The movie was a 1959 Paramount production.*

remembering people's birthdays. And he never sought any special privileges just because he was a great movie star. I remember one time Gable and a friend, Ray Hommes of Beverly Hills, wanted to take a look at Eldorado Country Club [a plush private desert club], but they were refused entrance at the gate because they weren't members. The gateman didn't recognize Gable, who could've identified himself and easily gotten into the club, but Clark didn't say anything, and so they left."

In the winter of 1959, Gable was still the acknowledged "King of Hollywood." The Number 1 table was reserved for Gable and Kay when they attended a party at Chasen's restaurant in celebration of the premiere of *Suddenly Last Summer*. Ordinarily, the table would have been reserved for Elizabeth Taylor, star of the film. But the respect given Gable was even greater than the respect given Taylor. The biggest stars of Hollywood were in attendance at the party. They, like movie fans everywhere, stared at Gable with an awe only reserved for the great.

10
Death of the King

GABLE, AT AGE 59, GREATLY ENJOYED the peace he had found at Palm Springs and at the Encino ranch, but he entertained no thoughts of abandoning his career. "When the public doesn't want me any more, I'll quit," said Gable. "The day they stop coming to see my pictures, I'll know they don't want me."

And in the late spring of 1960, faith in the public fondness for Clark Gable was underlined. Producer Frank Taylor offered Gable a bigger fee than he had ever received, a whopping $750,000 plus percentage of the profits—and $48,000 per week for each week of overtime shooting—to star in *The Misfits*. Gable's co-star was to be sex queen Marilyn Monroe. Her husband, the great American playwright Arthur Miller, wrote the screenplay. One of Hollywood's leading directors, John Huston, was named to direct. The fine supporting cast included Montgomery Clift, Eli Wallach and Thelma Ritter. It would be one of the most important film undertakings of all times. Taylor wanted Gable because he was "the only actor in the world who could express the essence of total masculinity that the leading role required."

United Artists budgeted *The Misfits* at $3.5 million, a high figure for a black-and-white motion picture. Producer Taylor, who had a long career as a book publisher, told a *Time* magazine reporter: "This is an attempt at the ultimate motion picture." He said each of the actors in the cast "*is* the person they play."

Huston and Taylor carefully lined up the best production talents available—the best cameramen, assistant directors, film editors, set decorators, and experts in sound, lighting, make-up and props. In all, the crew numbered more than 200.

During his years as a free-lance actor, Gable read many scripts, but found few he liked.

In 1959 and 1960, Clark and Kay played a lot of golf at Bermuda Dunes, where they owned a home.

United Artists planned extensive publicity. There would be much coverage of the production of the picture. A flow of articles was to deluge every newspaper in the country, and 200 national magazines. Word of *The Misfits* would travel on the airwaves of radio and television stations across the nation.

Overweight from months of leisure, Gable began preparing for the film. He dieted and exercised so he could better fit the role of Gay Langland, a tough but aging wild horse hunter who falls in love with a divorcee. Gable was excited about the film; it was a "strong role" and the picture had "something to say." It was said that Miller had conceived and written the script for Marilyn Monroe alone, but Gable had read the entire scenario and loved it. He not only relished his part, but was enthusiastic about the story as well. "I never select a part just for the part itself," he said.

As Gay Langland, Gable would play a roaming cowboy who loves the country life and the excitement of rounding up wild horses, which are called "misfits" because they are too small for riding. Langland initially sold the misfits as children's ponies, but his employer later sold them to dog food companies.

Gay Langland was a man determined to live his own life, refusing to give up his independence. His girl friend, Roslyn (Marilyn Monroe), was bothered by his contribution to the deaths of the mustangs. At the picture's end, out of his love for Roslyn, Langland releases a stallion he had succeeded in subduing after a fierce battle. He then quits horse hunting entirely.

Shooting for *The Misfits* began on July 18, 1960, in Nevada, a week after the Gables' fifth wedding anniversary. Accompanied by the Menascos, Kay and Clark left the Encino ranch early so they could celebrate their anniversary in Minden, Nevada, the town where they were married.

The Gables rented a large house on the outskirts of Reno, and made it cozier by bringing some of their Encino ranch furnishings with them. The children accompanied Clark and Kay. Much of the location shooting was done on a blistering hot, dry desert lake at Dayton, Nevada, about 50 miles from Reno. Temperatures reached an unbearable 110 degrees or more by afternoon. Alkali dust blew like rooster tails from desert winds or vehicles.

Although they lived not far from Reno's glittering gambling and night spots, the Gables seldom went into the city. Ernie Dunlevie, who visited with Clark and Kay for 10 days, said that one of the few times Gable went to town was to attend a party for Marilyn Monroe at the Mapes Hotel. "He looked out of place there," said Dunlevie. "He looked more natural sitting in the men's locker room with the guys at the club than he did in his own business."

Although he had slimmed down (he had lost 35 pounds), Gable found the filming of *The Misfits* strenuous. He worked harder than he had in years. There were several physically demanding scenes. In one, he roped mustangs from the back of a truck; in another, he singlehandedly roped and tamed a wild stallion and was dragged on the ground for several feet. In still another, he fell across the hood of a car and tumbled down to the ground, hitting it hard.

Probably the most exhausting scene for Gable involved being dragged 400 feet by a truck moving at 35 mph. A stunt man could have been used, but Gable was bored waiting around on the set. He insisted on doing the scene himself. Consequently, he suffered bumps and bruises all over one side of his body.

Another vigorous scene required that Gable sprint 100 yards several times in the 100-degree heat.

"Gable seemed to be under a strain during the movie," said Dunlevie. "They worked him hard. I visited him on location while he was filming a deserted cabin scene in which he picks up a big cement block, carries it, and puts it in front of a door for Marilyn Monroe to step on. They must've shot that scene 12 to 15 times. And it wasn't a fake block."

Monroe, on the threshold of a divorce from Arthur Miller, was in a

Eli Wallach, Thelma Ritter, Gable and Marilyn Monroe in a scene from The Misfits.

Marilyn Monroe, playing paddle ball in a bar scene from The Misfits, *drew laughs from Gable, Thelma Ritter, Eli Wallach and Montgomery Clift.*

state of mental anguish and collapse. She ingested heavy doses of drugs and frequently arrived late for shootings. Huston and the film crew were disturbed. Gable was upset, too. He had been punctual throughout his film career, had looked forward to working with a sexy, fiery leading lady like Monroe. But her tardiness disturbed him.

Monroe had great respect for Gable. Playing opposite him was a "dream come true," she said, adding that "When I was growing up, Clark Gable represented everything I idolized."

Shooting on *The Misfits* was halted on August 27 because Marilyn was ill and had to be flown to Los Angeles. She was admitted to Westside Hospital for treatment of acute exhaustion. Her physician, Dr. Hyman Engelberg of Beverly Hills, advised her to go to the hospital for medical treatment and a week's stay. Studio officials said that Marilyn had been working six days a week in the Nevada desert, where the temperatures had averaged 100 degrees. It was decided that all filming be suspended until her recovery.

Marilyn flew back to Reno on September 6, and shooting resumed. She continued to report late to the set—one time, as much as an hour-and-a-half—causing repeated delays in filming. On several occasions, she reportedly was indisposed or ill.

Although the shooting delays caused by Marilyn's health problems and her tardiness on the set were somewhat upsetting to Gable, he was cheered by the information he had learned in August: Kay was pregnant. "This time there will be no accident," she promised him. "And it will be a boy. I guarantee it!"

Gable was overjoyed by his imminent fatherhood, which was publicly announced on October. "Imagine a wonderful thing like this happening to an old guy like me," he said to friends. He looked upon it as somewhat of a miracle, reflecting upon the fact that he was 59 and she was 43. "It will be like starting all over again," he said.

Although the baby was not due until early spring, Clark and Kay spent a lot of time planning the infant's nursery and discussing its future. When Kay asked about the baby's religion, Clark left the decision to her. Clark had been baptized a Roman Catholic, his mother's faith, but his father was a Methodist. Kay had been baptized a Catholic and had been bringing up her own children in that religion. She wanted Clark's baby to be baptized a Catholic as well. "I knew you'd like that," he told Kay.

On October 5, the sky was so overcast that shooting was abandoned for the day. Gable used the free time to inspect Bill Harrah's famous collection of more than 300 antique and classic automobiles in Reno. He was impressed by the array of restored cars, particularly a beautiful Duesenberg roadster identical to the one he had owned in the early 1930s. On October 15, another filming delay, this time caused by the script girl, enabled Gable to do some duck hunting with Charles Mapes, owner of the

Mapes Hotel, at Mapes' private hunting preserve.

With location shooting finally completed on October 18, the entire film crew of *The Misfits* returned to Hollywood, where they were to shoot the interior scenes on the sound stages of Paramount Studios. Kay and the children flew to Los Angeles. Gable drove his Mercedes 300 SL the 477 miles back home; he did it nonstop in eight hours.

Back at the ranch, Gable spent all available time planning for the baby. He used a tractor to pull up citrus trees to make room for an addition to the house: the nursery.

The picture ran a week and a day beyond schedule, giving Gable an extra $56,000. His total guarantee for the film was raised to $806,000.

Gable viewed a rough cut of *The Misfits* on November 3, 1960. He liked it very much. All that remained to shoot was a retake of the last scene in the picture in which he is in a station wagon with Marilyn Monroe.

The next day, Friday, November 4, the last scene was shot. Gable did not feel well, but went to the studio anyway and played the scene without comment. A traditional studio party was held on that day to celebrate completion of the film. Gable did not stay for the festivities. He immediately drove home after telling the cast he was "taking off until the baby comes. This baby is a dividend. I want to be there to see him."

He had planned to fly to his hunting club immediately upon completion of the picture, but Kay discouraged it.

On the next day, Saturday, November 5, Gable started to change a tire on his Jeep at the ranch. He suddenly felt a gripping pain in his chest and dropped to his knees. Sweat broke out on his forehead, his face whitened. After a minute, the pain subsided. Clark was certain he had a virus. He tried to relax and, later in the day, walked his dog in the fields behind the ranch. He spent much of the evening playing with Bunker and Joan. The horseplay included wrestling on the floor.

When Gable awakened at about eight o'clock on Sunday morning, he told Kay: "I have a terrible pain. It must be indigestion." He had difficulty dressing himself. Alarmed, Kay went to call a doctor. He stopped her. "No, don't. This will go away in a while. I don't need a doctor." Kay, fearing he was having a heart attack, called a doctor despite Clark's wishes. Meanwhile, still in pain, Gable cancelled plans to see a horse Howard Strickling had arranged for him to look at and possibly purchase.

Dr. Fred V. Cerini of Encino arrived shortly. He looked at Gable and immediately called for an ambulance. In the meantime, the rescue squad of the Encino Fire Department was dispatched to give Gable emergency oxygen treatment.

Kay rode with Clark in a private ambulance to Hollywood Presbyterian Hospital. Immediately upon arrival, doctors ran him through a series of tests. Electrocardiograms revealed that the back of Gable's heart muscle had been damaged by two heart attacks, one sustained on Saturday and one on Sunday. He had suffered a coronary thrombosis—a crucial artery carrying blood to the heart had been blocked. Six nurses, two to a shift, were assigned to care for the movie star around the clock.

Dr. George C. Griffiths, who had been consulted by President Eisenhower's physicians when he suffered his heart attack in 1955, was called into the hospital to care for Gable. By Tuesday, two days after his second attack, Gable had regained sufficient strength to fill out an absentee ballot and cast his vote in the national election.

Doctors explained to Kay that the tenth day after a heart attack was generally crucial. Kay, who stayed in a hospital room across the hall from Clark, was at her husband's bedside often. She helped him pass the time as pleasantly as possible. They talked much about the baby. Once, he borrowed a stethoscope and listened to his son's heartbeat, remarking, "You must have Mr. America in there." Each day, Kay presented Clark with some of the messages he received by the hundreds. One of those was a wire from President Eisenhower urging him to follow his doctor's advice and "take it easy."

On November 16, 1960, ten days after he had been admitted to Hollywood Presbyterian, Gable's progress was so satisfactory that Dr. Griffiths suggested he withdraw from the case, and he did.

Clark and Kay dined together in his hospital room that night. She was delighted by his improved appearance; there was a peaceful expression on his face. At about 10:10 p.m., Kay herself started to feel ill. She kissed Clark and made an excuse to go to her room, saying that she would return right after the nurses got him ready for the night. "I love you," Kay said, hugging him tenderly. She left the room.

At 10:50 p.m., as Dr. Cerini opened the door to Gable's room, Clark glanced up and flipped the page of a magazine he was reading. His head fell back on the pillow—the King of Hollywood was dead.

Gable's death was unexpected. Even the doctors had been unprepared. He had responded well to anticoagulant drugs; daily electrocardiograms revealed that damaged tissue was healing; his cholesterol level was 258, only slightly above normal; he had not been on a diet high in fat content prior to the attack. All signs had been positive.

Dr. Griffiths said he believed that an extension of the original thrombosis had been the cause of death. Ten per cent of such cases end with a sudden and unforeseen death, he said.

Not since the passing of Rudolph Valentino, in 1926, had the film colony and the world so deeply mourned the death of an idol. Gable's death was front-page news in every major newspaper across the country. Moviegoers, for whom he had been a symbol for nearly three decades, felt a deep sense of personal loss.

Funeral services for Clark Gable were private. Kay had invited approximately 200 persons. The public was kindly asked not to attend the final rites, which were held on November 19. "There's nothing to see," the public was informed. Traffic was routed around the Church of Recessional, where the final rites were to be held.

The funeral ceremony was simple and dignified. The bronze casket was closed and covered by a blanket of garnet roses and a white rose crown. A flag, symbolic of Gable's military service, stood at one side. The funeral—with full military honors—was conducted by Chaplain Johnson West of March Air Force Base. A color guard and an honor guard of 10 airmen were in attendance. There was no eulogy for the actor who had been abundantly praised by millions in his lifetime. Services concluded with taps.

It was a bright and clear November morning. Wind stirred among eucalyptus trees that towered over the church, and leaves fell over the scene. Pallbearers Spencer Tracy, James Stewart, Robert Taylor, Howard Strickling, Eddie Mannix, George Chasin, Ray Hommes, Al Menasco and Ernie Dunlevie carried the casket from the church. Their destination was Forest Lawn Cemetery, 200 yards from the church.

A detail of five officers had been assigned to the Forest Lawn gates to cope with curiosity seekers. Hundreds of orderly fans armed with binoculars and cameras tried to spot some of the famous movie stars attending the ceremony—Adolph Menjou, Van Johnson, Jimmy Durante, Virginia Grey, Robert Stack, Randolph Scott, Ann Sothern, Lana Turner, Robert Wagner, Keenan Wynn, Norma Shearer, Jack Oakie and Loretta Young. Famous directors were there, too—John Ford, Frank Capra and Walter Lang—and producer David Selznick.

Three days later, Gable's body was laid to rest in the Great Mausoleum at Forest Lawn beside the tomb of Carole Lombard. Gable went to his grave wearing his gold wedding band and St. Jude medal, his last Christmas gift from Joan and Bunker.

Tributes from all who knew him, all whose life he touched, poured in for Clark Gable. All were from the heart. An editorial in *the Los Angeles Times* best summed up why Gable was King of Hollywood: "Rare human qualities Mr. Gable possessed in an unusual degree: virility graced by humor, good nature adorned by comprehension, an easy manner unspoiled by pretensions. To these engaging traits he added professional integrity and personal sincerity not easily found in the competitive atmosphere of the screen."

"It's hard to imagine a world without Clark Gable," wrote Louella Parsons.

Kay Gable, five months pregnant at the time of the funeral, was to face life without Clark Gable. She remained at the Encino ranch to await the arrival of her baby. It was the home in which she and Clark had shared five years and five months of happiness. Gable died as he was nearing the realization of a dream of many years—to become a father, to be financially secure and to be happily married to a woman he loved.

"Clark and I had so much happiness here together," Kay said in a January, 1961 interview. "Every room in this house is filled with love. There are so many wonderful memories. It's difficult to believe he isn't here, but it's something I must face. And I am, for his sake and the sake of the child, I am going to bear. If it hadn't been for this baby, I think I would've had a nervous breakdown."

An effort had been made to rush a final print of *The Misfits* for release by December 31, 1960, so it could qualify for the coming Academy Awards nominations. Taylor, Huston and Miller agreed that Gable had given a performance worthy of an Oscar. They wanted him to have the award, if possible. However, considerable editing and scoring still needed to be done. So *The Misfits* was not released until February 4, 1961. United Artists' distributors were very enthusiastic about the picture. They ordered 1,300 prints and decided to spend another half-million dollars on advertising, bringing the picture's advertising budget to $1 million. The final cost of the picture was $3,955,000. It was the most expensive black-and-white film ever made.

Montgomery Clift and Gable roped horses from the back of a truck in The Misfits. *Gable, at age 59, was called upon to perform several strenuous scenes.*

The critics gave high praise to Gable and the picture. "Gable, as Gay Langland, finally became the actor he might have been all along, if a part had come along to test him to this degree," said *Saturday Review.* "Gable has never done anything better on the screen, nor has Miss Monroe.

Gable's acting is vibrant and lusty, hers true to the character as written by Miller," reported the New York *Daily News*. "Gable really shines, meeting the brutal physical demands of the action with the masculine grace, ardor and dexterity of a young man," wrote *Variety*.

Arthur Miller was overwhelmed with emotion over Gable's acting. "Clark was in life a true hero, the only man in a heroic sense I ever knew. He was the only man I ever met who lived as my hero lived. I never knew anyone like him."

On March 20, 1961, at 7:48 a.m., Kay Gable gave birth to a healthy eight-pound boy by Caesarean section in the same hospital where Gable had died 124 days before. "Just what Pa wanted," said Kay. She watched the birth of her son (she had only been given a spinal anesthetic) in the reflection of a surgical lamp above her.

Richard Lang, who still had the Oscar Gable had given him many years before, came to the hospital and presented the Oscar to Kay. It was for her son, he said.

Kay named the child John Clark Gable. She knew that Gable opposed naming the baby "Clark," feeling that it would be too great a burden for any child to bear. A little less than three months later, on June 11, 1961, the baby was christened at St. Cyril's Catholic Church in Encino. Invited guests included Mr. and Mrs. Jack Benny, Mr. and Mrs. Robert Stack, Cesar Romero, Fred Astaire and Marilyn Monroe.

On August 4, 1962, Marilyn Monroe died from an overdose of sleeping pills. In *The Misfits,* her last screen appearance, Gable spoke these lines to her: "Honey, we all gotta go sometime, reason or no reason. Dyin's as natural as livin'. . . . Man who's afraid to die is too afraid to live, far as I've ever seen." In the closing of the film, as he drives off with Marilyn through the desert, Gable said: "Just head for that big star."

On the last day of shooting *The Misfits,* Marilyn Monroe said to Gable: "Do you know something? You're my hero. And I never had a hero before."

When Gable's estate was probated, it was revealed that under the law, though not mentioned in the will because he had not been born when it was drafted (September 19, 1955), his son would be entitled to half of his $912,000 separate property. The will left the community property to Kay. She was to receive $6,000 a month from his estate, which was valued at several million dollars, including future earnings from film percentages.

Gable's will gave Josephine Dillon the home in which she had been living for many years. She continued to live there, using the garage area as a drama studio until 1963 when she sold it and moved in with her cousin, Mrs. F. W. Hall, in Pasadena. Josephine died of pneumonia at the Rockhaven sanatarium near Glendale on November 10, 1971, at the age of 87.

After Gable's death, Josephine Dillon had been besieged by

newspapers, magazines and book publishers to reveal the "inside" story of Gable. "They want me to say something unflattering or sensational about Clark," she told reporters. "I refuse to say anything unkind about him. I can't think of anything belittling about Clark, and see no reason for defaming his good name." At the time of his death, she told the press: "Gable lived a life of great dignity, never compromised his standards, and never made a questionable picture."

Kay Gable remained at the Encino ranch until 1973, at which time she sold the house and the 20 acres on which it was set to real estate developers for a sum of $800,000, $750,000 more than what Carole Lombard and Clark had paid for it in 1939. The new owners subdivided the property into 38 half-acre lots selling for $42,000 to $60,000 each. The area became officially known as the "Clark Gable Estates." It included two newly-dedicated streets, Ashley Oaks and Tara Drive, named for the mansions in *Gone With the Wind*. The ranch home itself remained on two acres, with many of the trees retained. The developers sold the home in 1975 for $150,000. The new owners, a home builder married to a decorator —Barry and Valerie Eglit—have kept many of the Gable home's original features, particularly Clark's gun room, which they've dedicated as a memorial to him. It houses Gable photographs and other memorabilia. A wishing well where Gable proposed marriage to Kay is still intact. Tourists still cruise by the ranch and gaze wistfully at the plush $200,000 homes where Gable once tended his orchards and horses.

Kay Gable moved to Beverly Hills after selling the ranch. John Gable, now a handsome teen-ager, has broad shoulders and prominent ears. And, like his father, he likes cars and motorcycles.

The Clark Gable legend has endured. Clark Gable memorabilia— posters, theater lobby cards and photographs—is constantly being sought by collectors. Reruns of Gable films can often be seen on television. *Gone With the Wind* continues to be released again and again, and commands high admission prices. In 1975, Universal Studios undertook the making of a film, entitled *Gable and Lombard.*

What Louella Parsons said on the day of Gable's death still holds true: "There will never be another Clark Gable, nor another King of Hollywood."